'It's Not the Time You Have…'

'It's Not the Time You Have…'
Notes and Memories of Music-making with
Martyn Bennett

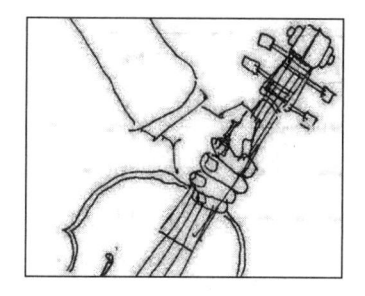

Margaret Bennett

Grace Note Publications

First Published 2006
Grace Note Publications
PO Box 26323, Crieff, PH6 2WX
Scotland
books@gracenotereading.co.uk

Also distributed by

Coda Music,
12 Bank Street, The Mound,
Edinburgh EH1 2NL
www.amazon.co.uk/shops/moundmusic
&
Footstompin Records,
17 Redford Drive, Edinburgh EH13 0BL
www.footstompin.com

ISBN 0-9552326-1-9

Copyright © Margaret Bennett
www.margaretbennett.co.uk

ALL RIGHTS RESERVED
No part of this book may be reproduced in any manner whatsoever, without express written permission from the publisher, except in the case of brief quotations embodied in critical articles and reviews.

All royalties from the sale of this book donated to
Bethesda Hospice, Isle of Lewis

To Kirsten,

May the road rise up to meet you,
May the wind always be at your back,
May the sun shine warm upon your face
And the rains fall soft upon your fields,
May God hold you in the hollow of his hands.

Philippians 1: 3 –
I THANK MY GOD EVERY TIME I REMEMBER YOU.

Sìth do Mhartainn Dhonn a' Bhealaich

'It's Not the Time You Have...'

"Think o' him through your heart...He's not far away, nor ever is..."
—Sheila Stewart, 2006

PREAMBLE

It's January, Celtic Connections again and this year Colin Hynd has programmed 'Martyn Bennett Day' for the first Saturday of the festival[1]. Everyone I meet, who knew Martyn or his music, seems to have a 'Martyn story'. He himself loved listening to, and telling, stories—except perhaps 'Martyn stories'. There were, of course, exceptions when he'd tell one that usually began, "you won't believe this..." and he'd laugh helplessly at some sit-com that seemed to have unfolded around him, creating the satirical humour that turns a situation into a story.

Whether invited or not, Martyn could give serious advice, and if you didn't seem to heed it the first time, you might get it again. I wasn't sure what I was supposed to do with one advisory comment offered me more often than was comfortable: "You must carry on doing what you do—it's important."
"Like what?"
"Recording people, folklore, writing, singing, passing on all that stuff you do—"
"Of course, I'll do that—what else would I do?" And I'd change the subject.

Recording other folk has been an integral part of my life—and of Martyn's. It all seems so ordinary to reach for a tape recorder, ask a few questions, listen to songs, music, tradition of any kind, or opinions about life in general, then transcribe the reels, cassettes, DATS or mini-discs of many voices. That's what a folklorist does. When you grow up with 'all this stuff' there's no need to analyse the process—you just take it for granted that 'everybody knows' you record these traditions so that they can be preserved for future generations, so that children and children's children will pass them on, sing the songs, play the tunes, or just

'It's Not the Time You Have...'

enjoy the language, the way of expression, the poetry, the people, the characters, the culture...

This is by no means an attempt to write a life story, but merely to record a few anecdotes shared by some of the folk who have been part of Martyn's world of music-making. While a number of them arrived by letter or email, most were recorded in conversations. They're simply put together for the enjoyment of those who knew Martyn, his music, his sense of humour, delight in the ridiculous, his intense perception, profound sensitivity and his warm compassion.

Margaret Bennett
Celtic Connections Festival
Glasgow, January 2006

'It's Not the Time You Have...'

"Only when we recognize that we are heirs can we truly be pioneers..."[2]

A TRIBUTE TO MARTYN

BRIAN MCNEILL, fellow music-maker:[3]

Martyn Bennett was a musician, composer, producer and pioneer who, in the short space of 33 years, made a contribution to Scotland's culture which was insightful enough to challenge the very core of his country's relationship with its own traditions. He did this by launching our national music on a series of highly significant journeys.

Significant in their commitment to experiment, Martyn's roads were radical ones, travelled through our traditional idioms, both Scots and Gaelic, with incredible virtuosity as staff, and with lightly worn scholarship as vade mecum.

Significant for his generation, this was a talent swept along upon a river of musical force, which tore down artificial barriers and made those traditions accessible to the young.

And lastly, significant for his country's artistic cohesion, his was a flight which soared high enough for him to see and reinforce the connection between many of Scotland's artistic topographies.

Born in Newfoundland[4], brought to Scotland as a young child, by the age of twelve Martyn was already winning piping competitions and showing the kind of virtuosity on the fiddle which would bring him not only the respect of his peers, but also of his elders. An early love of classical music was apparent, as was a bright, no-nonsense intellectual curiosity. His mother Margaret, one of Scotland's most brilliant folklorists, remembers him at a folk festival[5], aged four, peering into the mouth of an Inuit throat singer, trying to work out what could make her voice so different, and, on another occasion, aged seven, insisting on establishing for himself that it was the orchestral flautist and not the stage Papageno who was actually producing the notes of the Magic Flute.[6]

The musical education which followed took him to the Edinburgh City School Of Music, and then on to the RSAMD, where he studied violin under Miles Baster by day and slipped out to play traditional music in the sessions at night. Here he also met his beloved wife Kirsten, who was to have such a huge influence on his life. And here, at the RSAMD, he began to amass the musical arsenal which gave his compositions their distinctive voice.

At this point it should be made clear that a career as a classical violinist would have been well within Martyn's reach, but, while he loved classical music enormously, he was no fan of the professional milieu which surrounded it, feeling strongly that he could not be himself within that world. But then, by the end of his time here, I don't think any one genre could have imposed its limits upon him; it came as no surprise to me to hear that this master of the traditional and classical decided to do his Honours dissertation on the jazz violin of Joe Venuti.

I first met Martyn in the early nineties at the Tønder festival in Denmark, that great international crucible of the folk world. I'd just watched him playing his pipes with Wolfstone, a tremendous muscular folk-rock performance that drove three thousand people wild. He ended it in true rock star fashion by tearing off his shirt and throwing it into the audience, where it was promptly fought over by three determined teenage girls. The inevitable backstage session which followed was urgent, adrenaline-fuelled and mighty, and it was five in the morning before we paused to talk.

He wanted to know what made me tick, musically, and he proceeded to grill me. I don't remember much about my replies, but I do remember knowing—immediately—that my answers mattered, that I had to be honest with this wise old man of half my age. In return I asked him—and remember, this was long before my involvement here as Head of Scottish Music—about this place, the Royal Scottish Academy Of Music and Drama. When he told me, I said it didn't sound like much fun. He said I was wrong, it was a lot of fun, but the people who ran the place didn't seem able to tell anyone that.

After that it got to gentle jokes. We agreed that the old fogeys weren't the problem, it was the young ones you had to watch out for. We agreed that Scottish Opera was a reasonable Wagner tribute band. And how many folkies did it take to change a light bulb? One, and a hundred to mourn the passing of the old one...

The next time I met him was at Danny Kyle's funeral in Paisley. By then he was a recognised force. I'd kept up with his music, and I congratulated him on the CDs—and told him that I couldn't understand all of his music. He didn't even pause to think. Could I react to it?, he asked. When I said I could, he assured me that was more important, even if my reaction was negative. I assured him it wasn't and asked if he was getting a lot of negative reaction. He gave me a rueful grin and said 'The traddies'. I told him to remember that it wasn't the man who did the same as the man before who made it into the musical history books, and that if he was annoying the traddies he had to be doing something right, for there was an element among them which would always bleat against anyone who used the tradition as foundation stone rather than fossil.

For that is exactly what this remarkable musician and composer did. The late, great Hamish Henderson called Martyn's work 'This Brave New Music', and the important word in that fine blessing is 'new', for these important works never repeat themselves. Listen to 'MacKay's Memoirs', piobeareachd married perfectly to orchestra.[7] Listen to 'Hallaig', Sorley Maclean's voice given a new force that would inspire Gaelic children to learn his poetry from Martyn's recording. And above all, listen to his last two recordings, 'Glen Lyon' and 'Grit'.

The former, made when he was already very ill with the cancer which would eventually take him, demonstrates such understanding of the idioms of traditional song. Listen to the remarkable 'Cave Of Gold'—a song about a piper entering a cave. It was obvious to Martyn that any note of the modal melody could harmonise with any other. A second voice could have been pressed into service to highlight this, but reverb and digital delay do the job better and preserve the sparseness and the feel of the story.[8] The result is respectful, ethereal and beautiful— a dramatic soundscape created electronically around the organic treasure that is his mother's voice.

Then go to 'Grit' and take 'Liberation' —for many his masterpiece. What is so well demonstrated here is the certainty of the man's artistic vision. This isn't just music, it's a statement about Scotland.

The main performer here is Michael Marra—arguably Scotland's best writer of comic song. Martyn went straight past that fact to what he wanted—Marra's gravelled, pitiless working class voice. He used it to deliver line after line of remorseless steel-edged poetic scripture. The suspense of it is almost unbearable—until it explodes into the joyful release of rhythm above a minimalist melody. Thesis and antithesis, tension and release, the classic techniques of composition—and you'd have to be made of stone not to want to dance.

The loss of Martyn Bennett is tragic, mitigated for us only slightly by his own words, his self-imposed mission statement.
"It's not about how much time you have, it's what you do with the time that matters."

For what is the job of the artist? It's simple. The artist's job is to produce art. None of the rest of the stuff we do—the theorising, the teaching, the contextualizing—matters a damn without that one salient fact. Martyn Bennett did it in spades. He did his job with passion and commitment for as long as he humanly could, despite terrible illness, despite terrible psychological crisis, despite even the rage, which led him, at one time, to destroy his beloved instruments.

'Grit'. Never was an album title so appropriate. He was a working artist to the last, despite the cost to himself and those he loved, and his standards were never compromised by so much as a grace note. I am convinced that, a hundred years from now, he will be spoken of as a great pioneer, a liberator of our tradition from pose and sham, from narrow-mindedness and hypocrisy.[9]

KINGUSSIE—FIRST SET OF PIPES, FIRST GIG...

DAVID TAYLOR, history teacher at Kingussie High School, was Martyn's first bagpipe teacher. He looks back in this Email, January, 2006:

I first remember Martyn as a very tiny, excited, desperately enthusiastic wee boy with wide shining eyes. I've never seen anyone learn the chanter so fast. In his first lesson (1980) he mastered everything I gave him first time round—I probably gave him a month's worth of lessons in our first meeting. He was the most natural learner I've ever encountered—even making a practice chanter musical and playing grace note scales with perfect rhythm. It was only a few weeks before he was playing his first competition tunes on chanter. He had such light musical fingers when he played and even the hardest tunes flowed in such a natural, musical way. His impish sense of humour combined with his amazing talent meant he was always tremendous fun to teach. I think I looked forward to our lessons as much as he did.

Martyn was desperate to get on to the big pipes. I remember being asked by his Mum (in secret) to find a set—and nothing but the best would do, even though she had to save up for them! I went to my old piping teacher, Bert Barron in St. Andrews, who dealt in old sets of pipes. I explained that I was looking for a special set for this wee boy I was teaching and came home with an old set of full ivory-mounted Henderson pipes—so good that I was loath to pass them on. Never did a wee boy's eyes open so wide as when he got his first shot on them and, right from the start, Martyn played them as if he had been born with them under his arm, with that tone, control and flair which became a hallmark of his playing.

I often wondered about his natural—and uncanny—musicality, but it was ingrained in him. I remember the ceilidhs along at Margaret's house in Kingussie. There were always singers and musicians and Martyn just absorbed everything that was going on around him. He grew up with song and rhythm in his bones—music was just a part of what he was. He also played instinctive harmonies on the chanter and then the 'goose' to accompany his mother's singing. He loved playing tunes with the adults and used the goose for this first and then a lovely set of Colin Ross bellows pipes in C[10].

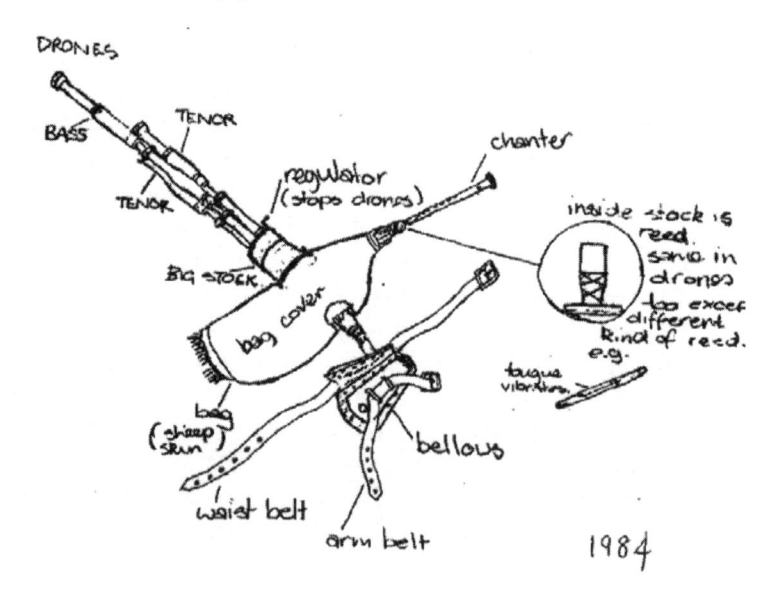

I also knew Martyn as one of my history pupils in Kingussie. He loved learning about the history of Scotland—always with a thirst for knowledge, always thinking about the people and their hardships. I took him on a school trip to Orkney to look at the old historical sites and again he loved seeing the old places and thinking about the people who had built them and lived there. It was there that I discovered another of Martyn's talents as an artist. I remember him lying on the grass producing a remarkably detailed and accurate sketch of one of the houses at Skara Brae[11]—quite oblivious to the other kids who were away off to play on the beach.

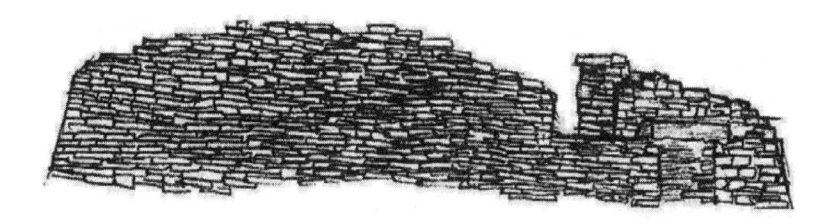

Many years later (1998, when he was playing a gig there) he sent me a postcard (still on my study wall) of the Ring of Brodgar in Orkney, which starts "I thought I would drop you a line from the inspiration behind that lovely music you taught me so many years ago...." That was Martyn—the history, the landscape, the music were all one seamless entity for him. (He also refers to the writing of 'MacKay's Memoirs' in that postcard.)

There is so much more I could say about Martyn, even though it is so many years ago that I first taught him. He is still the greatest talent I have ever had the privilege to teach. And yes, I do still have that card on my wall. It was very touching and one of my last memories of Martyn.

'It's Not the Time You Have...'

DOLLY WALLACE, storyteller, Perth, in conversation, Jan. 2006:

Dolly: Martyn did what must have been his first ever gig for me—and I didn't ever let him forget it. I always said that I launched him on the public scene for the first time! This was Dalwhinnie, when I was hosting Highland Nights in what used to be the Grampian Hotel, and he would be eleven at the time. That was 1982, and we did it for '82, '83 and '84. It was brilliant—every Tuesday night, from May to the end of September, half past seven to half past ten or after. I actually had four pipers—I almost had a pipe band! There was Martyn and I had Drew Sinclair and Christopher Thompson—one of them opened the ceilidh and finished it off. Sometimes Christopher and Martyn would play pipe duets, with harmonies. And of course you sang, so did Joe, and I would do a recitation or two.

  Those nights were special—and Martyn was unique. He was young—very young for a piper—he was small, beautifully mannered, and always smiling. And we had a wee dancer, she was six, wee Nicky, and if Martyn wasn't there, she was quite happy not to dance. She said to me one night, "Is Martyn coming?" And I said, "No," and she said "I'm not dancing! If Martyn's not playing, I'm not dancing—no way, just see if I am!" But I was only pulling her leg! And they must have been the most photographed pair in Britain at the time, because they

Kingussie Young Pipers

Donations will be greatly appreciated. Funds will go to buying reeds, books, tapes, etc.

Thankyou

'It's Not the Time You Have...'

were so small, so neat, and so sweet and pleasant. It was just all flashing lights round them! Oh, the tourists loved it.
Margaret: And did this cost a fortune?
Dolly: Huh! The hotel should have been paying all this, but I don't suppose anybody ever got paid. I don't think so— Hi-juice and crisps, and that was about it! But nobody seemed to be bothered; they were all enjoying themselves. So, I used to tease him I launched his career as a piper![12]

JOE MCATAMNEY[13], Glasgow, notes from a conversation, January 2006:
When we lived in Kingussie we used to go to Glasgow the odd weekend—me being a Glaswegian I'd need the occasional city fix. And I usually went to one of my old haunts, the car market in the Gallowgate, and Martyn always came with me—he just loved that, anything to do wi' getting your hands dirty, that was for him! Now we had this arrangement when we went places, I'd drive there, and Margaret would drive home—a pretty good deal, I thought. So, this Sunday night, we're driving up the old A9—this in the early 80s, before they did the by-pass at Killiecrankie—and Martyn told his mum that he'd done his homework in Glasgow when he was at the car market wi' me. Now that was news to me, so I goes, whit?
"Well," he says, "I had to collect a poem about an animal for Mr Morris's English class tomorrow, and I was really lucky because when we went to the toilets beside the car market, there it was, written on the wall."
"Really?"
"Yes."
"Eh'm, can you say it?"
"Yes, only I'm changing one word in the last line. It's got a word I don't think Mr Morris will like—bastards. So, I've been thinking about it—I think I have to change that word to beggars."
"Go on, then, say it." So Martyn starts reciting—

> No need to stand upon the seat
> The crabs in here they jump ten feet

'It's Not the Time You Have…'

And if next door you want to try,
Don't bother for the 'beggars' fly!

"You cannae say that, Martyn!" I says to him, trying to keep my face straight—and when she stopped laughing, I left Margaret to explain to him why no'!

Another late-night A9 drive north, early 80s, after some festival or other, Margaret was driving along playing a Bob Dylan cassette. I was probably nodding off, and Martyn was asleep on the back seat—or so we thought. There was virtually nothing on the road that time of night, bar these construction works. Anyway, the tape finished with Dylan singing 'It's a Hard Rain's Gonna Fall'—thon song we all used to sing in the sixties, whether or not we had a clue about the meaning—wi' all those disconnected lines. The tape clicked off, and the voice from the back seat says, "Do you know what that line means—a highway of diamonds with nobody on it?" He used to listen so intently to the words of songs as well as tunes, and Margaret says to him, "No. Do you?" "Well," he tell us, "what it really means is this: he's singing about a jewel carriageway, just like this road—see all these cats eyes—diamonds—and not a single car to be seen."

today my mummee kame bac from CANADA She brot me a yoocalaee. from CANADA. but I cood not plae it. but my mummee said that she wood teech me. I have a case for my yoocalaee.

The world through Martyn's eyes was full of surprises… He was probably on some amazing jewel carriageway and the rest of the world on an ordinary dual carriageway. And to think we used to tease him and tell him he only took up the bagpipes because he couldnae spell ukulele![14]

'It's Not the Time You Have...'

PEIGI (STEWART) BENNETT, Martyn's grandmother (Uig, Skye, and later Balquhidder), recorded in Glasgow, January 14, 2006:

Margaret: When we lived in Kingussie, did you not teach Martyn some Gaelic songs?

Peigi: Well he sang at the Mod, didn't he? He'd be eleven or twelve. And he was taking piping lessons from David Taylor at that time—oh, the Kingussie days are very vivid. David used to come around and they used to play... I'd be there for weeks sometimes, and the funny thing is that he use to ask me to tell him a bedtime story and then he'd go to bed with a drawing board and a big pad of paper and he'd draw and draw every evening before he went to sleep! And then, he used to read the Kilberry Book of Pibroch in bed, he'd write music in bed... I believe I bought it for him, remember, when he was about twelve and he was competing somewhere, I think Newtonmore. And he got a first prize and when he came home and he handed you a maroon colour Parker pen and he handed me a white one. That was him, spending his prize money on presents for you and me. He was always so generous—he certainly was. He used to think about other people, when most children of that age are dying to spend the money on themselves, but he always thought about other people first. And not very long ago, Margaret, when they spent a lot of time travelling between Edinburgh and Mull, he would always stop and see me, and if he had made a new CD he'd bring me a copy. I have a few of these CDs, and think it was something from 'Grit' he was playing on my CD player and he put this on to listen [laughs] I can hear him talking to himself saying, "Oh I can't hear the bass...", passing comments, not to me, but to himself, about sounds he was annoyed about. And the next time he came around, I think he was on his own, he was carrying this box and he put it on the floor and started unpacking it and then he set up that CD player there, with a lovely sound, a much better sound—and then he put on the CD and I just could not believe the sound! And it was only after he set it all up, he said, "Granny, *your* CD player is just rubbish!" [Laugh]

I have a lot wonderful memories of Martyn —I spent a lot of time with him, especially when he was little. Of course we always have the habit of singing lullabies when we put the children to sleep—we had a rocking chair, so did you.

Margaret: You told me one time Granny thought it'd be unheard of not singing to a little one! And the old people had a rocking cradle in the kitchen so even if Granny was at the stove or knitting she could rock the baby with her foot. Did Martyn have any favourite song?

Peigi: Oh, he liked *'Ba ba mo leanabh beag'*—if he was tired he's say, "Granny sing *ba-ba*…" But then he had his own little gramophone, didn't he? He used to run around and put on a record and turn it over [laughs]. He'd be singing 'Train on the Island', that was the one he used to listen all the time— he used to play it over and over again! That was the record you bought him wasn't it?[15]

Margaret: Well, not exactly! It was actually *my* record, a Folkways recording from the Smithsonian, sung by Joe Hickerson (he was the archivist there for years). I had this old record-player—I had before I was married, and he just wouldn't stay away from it—wee mischief, you couldn't turn your back to put the kettle on but he was off to the living room. I remember being wakened up one morning before six, to this blaring music—he'd gotten up, straight into the living room, but he'd turned it on full volume, so loud he frightened himself! He came running through the house crying for help—you couldn't help laughing at him! What had happened was, this old-fashioned thing had an ON-switch which was also the volume, and he'd turned it round completely! He'd be about two or three—anyway, Ian and I bought another, better one for the living room and we put that old one in his room with a few children's records. But it still didn't stop him sneaking ones from our collections—my old Joan Baez ones, Tom Paxton, Library of congress records, classical music, and

'It's Not the Time You Have...'

Na h-Oganaich, the MacDonald Sisters, Welsh Male Voice choirs, fiddle music—Ian had a quite a few. Anything! His other favourite was Dennis Brain playing Mozart Horn Concertos—he'd go round the house singing, "booom-bom-ba-bom-bom-ba-bom", being a French Horn! Funnily enough, I can't remember either of us thinking this was unusual—Ian played the violin and he has a really good voice; friends played music, so there was always music in the house. We probably thought every child did this.

Peigi: Then, in the summer, your dad and I would sometimes go to the Codroy Valley to spend the weekend with you and Martyn. And we'd all go over to old Allan Macarthur's house. There'd be pipes and accordions and fiddles going, and step-dancing. And Allan use to start talking about the old times. I was amazed at the old Gaelic songs he had, and the words he knew. I don't believe he could read Gaelic. The whole family could play, sing, dance—all the children would be part of it—not just Martyn, but all of them. Yes, they were all part of it.

Then of course [in later years] he spent a lot of time with us in Balquhidder. He used to love to walk in the hills—and when he was younger, he'd go with us to Glenconon (Skye)—he loved Glenconon. I remember taking him to the end of the glen and then he went on by himself, around five miles. He loved climbing, he'd take a sandwich and be gone all day. And of course the Cuillins. Then, Kirsten would go to the hills with him too, and go camping. You can hear that in his music.

'It's Not the Time You Have...'

EDINBURGH—AT HOME WITH FRIENDS...

CATHAL MCCONNEL, flute player extraordinaire (Fermanagh and Edinburgh)—conversation after a concert of Martyn's music in the Royal Concert Hall, Glasgow, January 14, 2006:

Cathal: I was between houses and you and Martyn were living up at Strathearn Road at the time and I was there for three months. Now, how many years ago was that? Shona was born in '87, so it must be 18 going on 19 years ago. How did we all get along together? Ah, it was great! Martyn was still in school, and of course you and I, we lived at opposite ends of the day—you get up VERY early! And I'd say we were all good pals—yes, definitely, without question. We'd laugh a lot! We get on fine. Oh, there were some, eh—[laughs], there was one time I came crashing in, I think— yes. I came crashing in at 4 o'clock in the morning and was noisy! [laugh] And you woke up! [laugh] But there was never any problem really—no—no cross words; I can hardly remember anything, even with Martyn.

I remember he used to come from the school at 4 o'clock, and the school bag'd be thrown down. And I'd have the kettle on, and Martyn'd be gone for the biscuits and he'd say, "McConnel has been there before me!" There'd not be any biscuits left! I always like biscuits with my tea and coffee, you know, I always like that. We used to have good fun, that way!

But another time I stayed, it might have even been before that, when Martyn was still at school. It was when you were away, America, I think, I stayed with Martyn. So it was just the two of us, yes that's right. And I think he did all the cooking. [laugh] Yes, he did, because I'm useless in the house, I don't cook at all! And he says, "Now, mammy, you left Cathal to look after me and I have to tell you something: I looked after him," he says, "cooked everything for him!" [Laughter]

'It's Not the Time You Have...'

```
LOTHIAN REGIONAL COUNCIL          EDUCATION

                                  Director  W. D. C. Semple.
                                  Divisional Education Officer
                                  (Edinburgh)  G. E. Ferguson.
                                  40 Torphichen Street, Edinburgh EH3 8JJ
                                  Telephone 031-229 9292

                                  Our reference   E/A/AD
                                  Your reference
     Mrs Bennett
     49 Balcarres Street          Date   16 April 1985
     EDINBURGH
     EH10 5JQ


     Dear Mrs Bennett
     SCHEME FOR EDUCATION OF MUSICALLY GIFTED CHILDREN

     Following the final auditions for admission to Broughton High Music
     Unit I am pleased to inform you that Martyn is being offered a place
     from 30 May 1985(this is the start of the new academic year at Broughton
     High School). I should be grateful if you would let me know as soon
     as possible whether or not you wish to take up the place.  If you do
     accept, Mr Scott, the Head Teacher, would be pleased to see you to
     discuss more detailed arrangements for Martyn's admission and I
     would suggest you telephone the school (031 332 7805) for an appointment.

     Since the school is over two miles from your home Martyn will be
     entitled to travelling expenses between home and school.  Please
     complete and return the enclosed application form.

     Yours sincerely


     DIVISIONAL EDUCATION OFFICER
```

But Martyn was very special person in my book—of course we had a very deep musical relationship, playing together. It was wonderful that I had the privilege to be living in your home at that time, to be with Martyn—I mean those were happy days, you know… We were similar in the sense that he liked doing creative things with the music and variations and all that. And one of the pieces that we played a lot together was 'The Morning Dew'. And indeed Martyn was thinking of recording me at one time—we were supposed to be recording, doing something together, but it never came about.

'It's Not the Time You Have...'

Being with him so much, there something I noticed with Martyn—he was very much an individual person. He was Martyn—okay, you might have been his mother! But he had a definite personality, very independent—and if he didn't agree on something, oh you knew. But I can't remember any falling out—never! No, not at all, we all laughed a lot!

You would come home, and first thing you'd hear'd be the two whistles! We'd be playing, playing, there'd be no stopping the tune to speak—but he had this kind of a nod, and a look like you knew he wasn't ignoring you! Then I used to tell to you, "Martyn's about the only person who speaks my language." [laughs] Indeed, I remember... Well, we're kindred—kindred spirits, you know. Because with a lot of other musicians, they don't understand me—they see me as a 'way out there' musician, and of course Martyn was a bit like that; there's people who couldn't understand him.

I recall one particular thing, oh, I wish I had a recording of it! You weren't there, it was just Martyn and me, and Martyn was playing the pipes and the late Gordon Duncan was playing the pipes... it was wonderful... amazing—they were both brilliant.[16]

Then when you think of that time, as well as playing the pipes, Martyn could play the flute, he could play the piano, fiddle, viola, and he could sing—

Margaret: Oh, we'd tease him he could get a tune out of a saw or a bicycle pump—that's true! But I remember, Cathal, you bought him an ocarina one time—brought it back from some tour or other. Delighted he was, [laughs] but next thing, he's playing Handel's 'Arrival of the Queen of Sheba' on it!

Cathal: I remember we used to have long conversations, mainly musical, you know. Like I mean, for Martyn, I suppose I was a kind of father figure, like on the music thing. He was picking up things off me—and I was picking things off him. Oh, I would certainly say with Martyn that our main conversations were music—I don't think I talked to him very much about school or anything else, you know! I admired his modern

'It's Not the Time You Have...'

mind, his ways of looking at things. We definitely learnt from each other. Like, I remember playing a piece of music I called 'Farewell Waverly Park'—I made it when I moved out of Waverly Park. And Martyn helped me on some of that tune, you know—he suggested a note that I hadn't thought of, and it was right. It was a complex tune anyway. And I remember another time we were going over this tune and we were trying to figure it out, and it was a Scottish tune—[sings: dum-da-dee-dadee-dum-da-dee...] and it was tricky, and it was slightly different the second time and I remember having a deep conversation.

And one of the pieces that we played a lot together was 'The Morning Dew', but I can't remember teaching him the 'Swallowtail Reel'[17], no... 'The Morning Dew', yes, but obviously we played much more than that. But 'Morning Dew' was a favourite because it'd be different every time, crossing over with the harmonies, reading each other thoughts, anticipating each other's moves, if he went up, I'd be down, never seemed to 'crash', and sometimes we'd start to laugh in the middle of it—we'd make it to the end of tune, different every time! We'd a great understanding. Oh, him and I were definitely kindred spirits— yes, very much. Definitely,

And I would say he was the first person really to do all this modern music and put his own backing together. He was away ahead of his time, really. Yet he was rooted in tradition, very much so—of course he got it from you. And even after listening to the concert today [with MacFalls Chamber and the Scottish Opera Orchestra] you can hear the traditional stuff coming through. Even in his modern pieces you can hear he was very deeply rooted in that, I mean. You can still hear it, although—

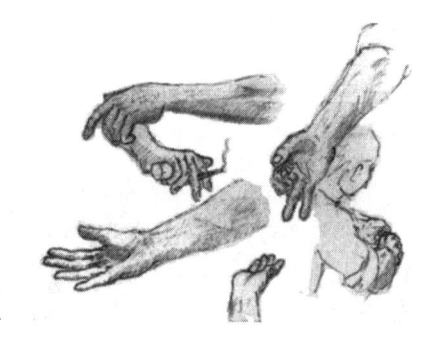

[laughter] you'd be listening hard when you hear some those pieces. But even in them, I can still hear hints of tradition. Of course he got it from you and you probably got it from your people and all that, so I think it was naturally in him—I think it's in the genes.

But the thing you've probably forgotten, Margaret, he did a gig with the 'Boys of the Lough'—we had him as a guest… he was very hippy at that time, his hair, very sort of—Anyway, we got him up on stage and of course he went down a storm. People just loved him! He was one of the most spectacular people that we had on stage—well in the first place he was young, and in the second place, young people attract young people. And he was talented. Of course, if a person is young and good they generally come across better than someone who is old and good!

I mean, he was extraordinary, very important. To achieve so much in his short life… an extraordinary man—but I knew him as a little boy.[18]

Mrs. John MacLellan — March — by J. A. MacLellan, 1949

BUNTY MACLELLAN, wife of the late Capt. John MacLellan (former Head of the Army School of Piping), Martyn's piping teacher in Edinburgh—in conversation on January 5, 2006:

Bunty: I don't think John would ever have been in the army but for the piping— Well, there's an old saying that says "A piper is married to his bagpipes and lives in sin with his wife!" So if you marry a piper you have to accept that there's no way round it. When I married I knew nothing about piobaireachd—absolutely nothing, and so I had to learn. And now I can talk about piobaireachd at the drop of a hat.

'It's Not the Time You Have...'

It was Dr Kenneth MacKay[19] that said to John, you must take this boy [Martyn]—that must have been just when you came to Edinburgh first. And this came about because, when John and I went up north, Rogart, the Northern Meeting in Inverness, and so on, we used to like to stop in Newtonmore and visit Dr Kenneth MacKay and his lovely wife Margaret. Kenneth used to run the Laggan School of Piping—he was a great enthusiast and he and John were great friends. Well, it was on one of those visits that we heard about Martyn. And then Kenneth wrote to John and told him that he simply *had* to take him—in case anyone else would ruin his playing!

Martyn would come to the house, on his way home from the school. You know, he would be up there with John, doing his lesson, and then he'd come down and he always stood there, in the kitchen, with his back to the counter. I'd give him tea and clootie dumpling or something like that—he loved clootie dumpling! And he would talk about anything except piping—he was so interested in everything—everything. I remember John used to tell to make sure and go straight home after his lesson, because he used to stop and look at things on the way and get home hours later!

Margaret: Like the time he stopped to watch the fire or when he sat on the Royal Mile to draw St Giles Cathedral—this very picture.

'It's Not the Time You Have...'

Bunty: And John said that Martyn was his last pupil and his best—that's right. That's exactly how it was—it gave him great pleasure, oh, indeed yes.

ANNA WENDY STEVENSON, Edinburgh, recorded in February 2006:

Anna Wendy: I was fifteen when I met Martyn and I don't think I'll ever forget it. I was in the Edinburgh Youth Orchestra and we used to meet at Easter—they'd take a week, and have a week rehearsal and it was very intensive.[20] And I was in the second violin section, and Martyn was the leader. And during break-time everybody would go off and buy their bags of crisps and Cadbury cream eggs, and go off and do things. And I remember feeling I wasn't managing to get my head around a certain bit of music so I thought I'd stay and practise and I'd hoped that nobody else would stay. But Martyn was staying, he was also practising, but he didn't need to practise—he was just playing around. Then he just started speaking to me and asked had I seen these before—it was some low whistles and I hadn't seen anything like it. And he told me about Kingussie … where it was, and he was obviously wanting to talk to somebody just about his excitement about where he'd been living, and about music. So he played me these whistles, and I was absolutely entranced—and of course I thought he was the bee's knees! I always liked traditional music, and there's traditional music in my family, but you know when you've got moments in your mind that have definitely made such an impression that it's led you in a certain way—well that was definitely one of those moments. It made me feel very excited because I remember him talking about communities, and people getting together, and how much fun it was playing music. My heart just ached because I wanted that. And here I was in an orchestra—but at least he was in the orchestra as well![21] So it was nice to know that there were people interested

'It's Not the Time You Have...'

in the same things. He just seemed to give me a window into a world that he lived in, and the music that he loved—I mean he loved classical music as well; he just loved it all, and it was absolutely inspiring.

Margaret: So, there were no boundaries, in a sense, either within the home or in the community, and because you come from a very musical family, was this one of the aspects you had in common?

Anna Wendy: Absolutely, and to me family is very important and when you're a young person, to meet somebody else who has similar values means a lot. I was struck by the fact that he was very able, obviously extremely clever, but none of his sensitivity was compromised—and that's such a rare thing, and I was very tuned into that. That's what I've been brought up with—to have high standards, and obviously to master your instrument, but never to the detriment of sensitivity. And the feeling aspect—the feeling for the music—that was something that I knew right away, that I shared in common with Martyn.

Margaret: I remember you saying your grandfather could take hours to explain something that you thought could be explained in five minutes—because he really wanted you to understand. And yet, don't you think it tells years later?

Anna Wendy: Yes, definitely. I mean the thing that we all have in common is, music is life, and life is music. And with my Grandad, in order to explain a musical ornamentation, he might start talking about lace making in Rumania, and then show me a book of photographs and then start telling me of the wonderful style of photography, then architecture. My Grandad was also so fascinated by poetry and words. And Sorley MacLean, and all these names, they all crossed over and I knew—I mean, I remember Martyn just rambling away to me, and I was quite shy, and he would just be mentioning people in his life—about you, and when he mentioned Sorley MacLean of course that made me feel very excited because on my Grandad's wall was a portrait drawing of Sorley MacLean.[22] So our families were bound by similar interests

'It's Not the Time You Have...'

and by people in common—and people are so important. I think that Grandad's way of looking at things from a very world, universal perspective, and trying to relate things together is 'very Martyn'.

Margaret: Little wonder you'd feel so comfortable, so at ease.

Anna Wendy: Absolutely, yes. He was very inspiring—a lot of people would be inspired by him, well have been, obviously, and I'm definitely one of them. Also I felt this because he had been so supportive to me—for example, when he heard the recording that I had done with my grandfather, and he sat in the sitting room and said to my Dad, "Why is Anna Wendy not just doing this? This is wonderful, this is so special—this is the thing, THE THING!" And he valued it. The musical collaboration that I've done with my Grandad is really unusual in some respects, but I think it could be very misunderstood because it takes a certain kind of understanding—and some folk could miss the point. But Martyn knew the point immediately; he really did, and had great affinity with it. He thought it was very valuable and liked it a lot—and that meant the world to me.

'It's Not the Time You Have...'

Margaret: But he knew also that you had a similar understanding of his music—he really knew that.[23]

Anna Wendy: Sometimes I just wish that I could spend every day with my Grandad! [laughs]

Margaret: I can understand that entirely! But it's not just about being with this one special person, perhaps it's more about bringing all these generations with you and sharing them via your music with others and via your own personality. It's just without barriers, without anything to mar it, for you know your Grandad's never going to spoil it ever, and that's hard to find in any other relationship in our lives—so maybe it makes what you have as close to perfection as is possible in a relationship?

Anna Wendy: Absolutely! It's interesting, because this whole thing about families, it's something that's accepted much more in the Highlands than here, you know, it's understood that that's a natural thing. And maybe down in the Lowlands it's not yet accepted, but I think that we just have to be strong, and say, "no way, I am proud of my family, and I care about them and I want to do things with them, and what's wrong with that?"

Margaret: Exactly. We now seem to live in a society where, in general, people may be more inclined to read a book about ancestor worship or about North American Native people and their continuum of family and say, 'Oh this is cool,' and they'll bring it in a kind of new-agey way without realising that it was ours all the time. Anna Wendy, I think what you say about your grandfather is so important—you make me realise that, when it comes to valuing tradition and culture, this grandparent-grandchild aspect is perhaps even *more* crucial than the parent-child link because we (as children, no matter what age) are less likely to accept dictates from parents than grandparents. It is also the fact that, as children, we feel that, when it comes to relationships, even parents can let us down, make us doubt, or not give us the reassurance or security we seek. But, once in a while, it is found in a *grandparent* with whom that rare and special bond exists—and when it does, it represents the essence of what we seek in life's relationships—someone in whom you have absolute trust, who NEVER lets you down, who, when they offer advice you know it is in your very best interest and not out of some parent-child agenda. Crossing *two* generations makes it different. This is exactly what Martyn had with his grandmother, Peigi, and what I had with my own grandfather, John Stewart (*Seanair*, we called him)—and although I got most of my songs from my mother, nevertheless it is to Seanair I attribute the deepest depth of understanding of my culture and tradition. Yes, I got an enormous amount from both my parents, and my other three grandparents, but in Seanair there was something that defied definition or description, like one of life's rare gifts. That total trust and a glorious bond that is so complete, so easy, so natural that it is sometimes, maybe often, misunderstood or regarded in a sort of 'how odd, how weird, sort of way. And only the individuals who have it really understand that it is nothing to do with dependency or some kind of family neurosis, it is a very special gift you know that very few people have because you come across so few who instantly recognise it—and Martyn recognised it in you just as you did in him.

RAYMOND ROSS, playwright, journalist and editor, Edinburgh. Email, January, 2006:

I think I first met Martyn in Sandy Bell's with Margaret and Hamish (Henderson), sitting at the table of an afternoon playing the pipes, part of the craic. He was maybe about 14 and had already composed a pibroch, was thought highly of by Sorley (Maclean) and Hamish. He was quite a quiet, shy boy but obviously highly talented and extremely personable. Sessions like that one became part of the fabric of Bell's and Martyn became

'It's Not the Time You Have...'

known as 'Margaret Bennett's son'—very soon to be reversed to Margaret becoming 'Martyn Bennett's mother'!

I remember slipping a wee story into The Scotsman Diary about Martyn busking on Princes Street in full Highland dress and not making more than a few bawbees. So, he went down the next day in jeans and T-shirt with a sign propped up against his pipe case "Saving up to buy kilt". He made some serious busking money from that—though he had several kilts at home. I liked that, the way he played the game. It reflected his attitude to life, I think, and to music.

Martyn was never hidebound; but was eclectic and adventurous which is probably why I asked him if he'd be interested in composing music for a play I was writing 'The Haunting of Billy Marshall'.[24] Billy was a 17th century gypsy king in Galloway (Hamish had prompted me to write about Billy) who'd reputedly lived till be was 120 years old. Martyn did a great job ('Suite for Billy Marshall' I think he called it in its own right) and played it multi-instrumental live on stage at the Fringe (Netherbow Arts Centre) and a Scottish tour (this was 1991) which took us to Kirkcudbright where Billy's buried. I still have a pic of Martyn and the cast at Billy's grave—the lot of us looking just a wee bit hung-over...

Martyn was informed by tradition but always sought to build on that. Some of the more staid forms, especially the drawing room sort, of music and song made him laugh, a kind of irreverent giggle he couldn't contain. I think he always wanted to shake things up a bit—which he did.

He played a couple of times at the Heriot Watt Edinburgh University Celtic Supporters' Club annual dinner ('The Tommy Burns Supper') and nearly blew the rafters off the venerable debating hall in Teviot House. He was acclaimed. He liked reaching audiences outwith the 'folk scene' and though he did his 'club mixes' that was never really him either—well, not the whole of him. I remember a Scotsman interview with him during the 'dreadlock period'. After reading it I said to him—what the hell was that all about? He said, "I know! Did I really say that stuff? I don't understand a bloody word of it either!"

I think he was always on the move musically, always sounding things out, but always grounded in the genuine—in the 'carrying stream' as Hamish would have it. But he wanted a music for the 21st century. He was about opening new doors and if that meant knocking down a few walls or tanning a few windows in the process, so what? Or rather, so be it.

He had the face of an angel and the grace-notes too. But he had the devil in him. Thank God.

THE SCOTSMAN, Diary, September 2, 1987
'Paying the piper'

There's a lot of psychology in this street-busking business; and young Martyn Bennett, a piper of some repute, is hereby nominated for the Diary's Fringe Benefits Scheme. Wearing the kilt and brogues, he found himself jostling for space in Edinburgh's Princes Street with other similarly-clad pipers as the Great British and Overseas Public swarmed past. His reward for a day's labour: £1.50.

Next day, Martyn put aside the tartan and wore jeans and a shirt when he took his pipes back to Princes Street. But he placed a notice on his open bagpipe case: Saving Up for Kilt. That day he took £35! (It's thought that he actually has three kilts in his wardrobe at home, but never mind.)[25]

Note from Hamish Henderson, Edinburgh 27 October 1995

Dear Margaret,

Welcome home! The enclosed articles about Martyn appeared on the same day in the Scotsman and the Herald respectively. He's appearing with me at the 'Six Towns Festival' (i.e. the Potteries Festival) this weekend, but I imagine I'll be back in Auld Reekie before you. I'm sure we have plenty to tell each other.

Love, Hamish.

PS I'm afraid the organiser of the 6 Towns Festival has rather gone over the top describing me—see leaflet enclosed!

'It's Not the Time You Have...'

[handwritten musical notation dated Dec. 1984, inscribed: "Martyn Bennett dedicated to Hamish / A great man and friend. Henderson"]

JOY HENDRY, Editor of *Chapman*, Edinburgh. Email, January, 2006:

I will never forget meeting Martyn for the first time, or nearly the first time, on 4 July 1985 when we all bundled aboard a bus to go to Langholm to protest about the Council's refusal to grant permission for the Jake Harvey MacDiarmid memorial (4 June, 1985).[26] At 9.30 in the morning, waiting for the crowd to assemble in Edinburgh's George Square, Martyn was sitting half in a hole in the ground, where workmen had been digging, tuning his pipes and playing away quite unselfconsciously. He looked about 11 at the time. I think I had heard him play at some Reading before, but liked him immediately for his open good nature, and was amazed at the quality of his playing. But immediately I had the impression of a boy quite at one with his instrument, and completely at one with whatever he was playing. Even then, he had a very special quality which shone brilliantly out of him, but unselfconsciously. There was almost no sense of ego.

From then on, he was a natural choice for any event I was organising. He was willing, and obviously very committed to literature, and on each occasion his contribution was brilliant, but unobtrusive. Gradually, I came to realise just how talented he was, as I heard some of his own contributions. I remember you at the Celebration of Women concert, talking briefly about how individuals develop talents and some of the difficulties encountered in the process, saying: "And when my son asked for a set of pipes, should I have given him a bit of plumbing?"—or some such—in a nice rhetorical flourish![27]

'It's Not the Time You Have...'

Martyn was, as I said, clearly committed to art in all its forms, and to helping and working with other artists. He also had an acute political sense—hence his love of Hamish and other poets of that generation who weren't afraid to be 'political'. He also had an acute sensitivity to words. Working with the words of the likes of Hamish's poetry gave him a structure to let his imagination fly—which it did—a sounding board on which to try his skill. I think he went through a period when this was in overdrive—just one of the stages a gifted musician and composer like Martyn was bound to go through—but he learned to temper this with judgement, his own natural restraint, reticence and discipline reasserting itself as he gained in maturity.

Martyn and I share a real shyness. When we were together on something we both tended to get on with what we had to do. But when we did talk, and I remember especially standing outside the Saltire Society premises at the launch of Greentrax's Hamish event, having quite a long talk. We talked then about his illness which at the time was in remission, and his hopes for the future. He had a clear, unsullied view of the future—remarkable considering what he'd been through. He was unpretentious and easy to get on with. I never ever noticed him, at whatever age, ill at ease with anyone. For him it was clearly quite natural to be in the company of Hamish [Henderson], Sorley [MacLean], Norman [McCaig], or whomever.[28] He behaved as an equal to all of us, but without being presumptuous or 'show-offy'.

His original compositions are a wonderful marriage of past, present and future in a glorious ménage à trois. The absolute ground of all his own music was the tradition he'd been imbued with from an early age. It was the solid platform from which he was able to do so many quite incredible and original things, all of which contained so many references, echoes, and above all the formal discipline of the tradition. Clearly his ties to family were very strong, and one of the reasons he was so generously willing to participate in literary events (for which he was almost never paid) was his sense of community. It was that sense of the literary community as emblematic of the wider Scottish, indeed world, community, which motivated nearly all of us.

Without his background and intimate knowledge of tradition he would almost certainly have composed, but not so well, or, ironically, so originally, as he did. Martyn understood the paradox of originality, that there is no originality which is not informed by the thorough grounding I speak of above. You have to subject yourself to that 'something greater'—in his case a thousands of years old one—in order eventually to reach and discover your own voice. Martyn understood that implicitly and explicitly—and at an amazingly early age. Most of us go through a prolonged stage of unbearable selfishness and egotism before we get to that place.

Most of all I remember Martyn for his willing, open, good nature and his generosity and genuine humility—though I think he was well aware of the extent of his own talent. He was quite unassuming, but with a wonderful sense of peace and composure about him. I remember Bobby Campbell, the Scotsman journalist (who died, sadly), presenting him quite aggressively as a 'genius'. I think he was right. We have lost a truly original and wonderful talent.

ANGUS FARAQUHAR, Director of NVA[29], Glasgow. Email, January, 2006:

I first heard Martyn play at an early Beltane on Calton Hill, probably in the late eighties, it was the early years of the re-initiation, attended by a few hundred hardy souls and each year an amazing mixture of musicians pitched up to play anywhere between midnight and seven in the morning, usually in driving rain...

'It's Not the Time You Have...'

Martyn, in his late teens, piped for four performers doing early Scottish dancing and the big surprise is what a serious boy he was on that night, great concentration in wild circumstances, playing with such a fluidity and confidence.[30] He seemed much older then than he did a decade later!

As far as tradition is concerned, the thing about all really great musicians is that they read 'tradition', not as a straightjacket or a mantle to carry on, but as a living, continuous form, whether full of flights or cul-de-sacs. Martyn had the natural ability to make something his own, to give a tune a resonance that could simultaneously link it to the past while being unmistakably of this time.

When I asked Martyn to do the Glen Lyon bit for 'The Path', I don't remember if I knew before or after that Martyn (or Margaret) had had such a strong link to the area, but asking him to place the famous Glen Lyon lament as a key point on the upwards route of The Path event in 2000 was a really important part of that work.[31] His fiddle playing, with Margaret's plaintive singing, had a profound impact on many who heard the track, positioned by a small rebuilt shieling at 1,200 feet. I often walked past people standing or sitting just crying or staring into space. It sounds like a cliché, but that's the simple power the music had. I sent Martyn CDs of the music done by two other musicians on the hill, the singing bowl players from Kathmandu and the beautiful voice of Ani Choying Drolma and I know he listened to them often when he was ill at that time.

Like anyone who knows Martyn, you just feel proud in whatever way to have had his creativity as part of your journey; no sorrow attached to that, as the songs, and his playful attitude, aligned with breathtaking skill, will carry well beyond this time.

'It's Not the Time You Have...'

FESTIVALS, JAUNTS AND FIRESIDE YARNS...

SCOTT GARDINER, singer 'bothy loon', Forfar. Email from Edinburgh, January 2006:

I had met Martyn a few times at the Keith Festival, but it wasn't until we found ourselves on the Aly Bain Young Champions Tour (1990) that I spent much time in his company. I remember him being cheery and sociable, doing very funny impersonations of others on the tour, and giving me my first proper taste of alcohol.

It was 2002 and onwards before I met him again. He had to come to Edinburgh for medical treatment a fair bit, and when he wasn't able to go home to Mull, him and Kirsten would bide at Margaret's house. I helped Margaret with her garden back then, and he would always have something knowledgeable or enthusiastic to say about various plants or trees or improvements we could make. It didn't take much to bring out the pernickety crofter in him.

I probably know more about Martyn from what I've heard (both the music and others' thoughts) and read, than from the limited time I spent with him. He touched the lives of so many through his amazing talent and likability. I'll remember him for his welcomingness, his thrawness and his good humour. And as a man who made you wish you were a wee bit more like him, and a wee bit less like everyone else.

JEAN URQUHART, The Ceilidh Place, Ullapool[32], between the winter solstice 2005 and the first day of spring 2006—extracts from a letter, a phonecall and a poem:

Dec. 2005,
Dear Margaret,
Like everyone who met him or knew of his wonderful gift, I felt Scotland lost a very special star ... (And yet) Martyn lives on in so very many young musicians for whom he was a real hero—
From all of us at the Ceilidh Place—

'It's Not the Time You Have...'

By telephone, March 13, 2006, reflecting on the Celtic Connections 'Martyn Bennett Day', in particular the Piece for String Quartet, Percussion, and Scottish Smallpipes in C[33]:

Jean: I was at both concerts in Glasgow on January 14—I wouldn't have missed them! Marvellous! You know, Martyn had our first ever world premier here at 'The Ceilidh Place', in 1996. I was on the Arts Council at that time, and on that very day I had a meeting in Edinburgh and I knew I wouldn't get out till 5. But I also knew the concert was starting at 8 so at least I'd catch the premier because that was to be played in the second half. So off I set.

Margaret: Edinburgh to Ullapool is some drive!
Jean: And it was a beautiful evening when I screeched over the gravel where they were standing having drinks at intermission. But they'd played it in the first half! And Martyn said to me, "Oh, don't worry, Jean." At the end of the concert (after they had played string quartets by Hayden and Schubert) Martyn came out to the front and said, "Jean Urquhart missed the premier, so, if nobody minds we'll play it again. And if you don't want to stay, then that's fine, you're very welcome

to leave." Of course nobody left—they would have sat through it ten times!

Margaret: Jean, your family have been on your own challenging path to travel—the poem composed by your husband on the death of a son is so apt.[34] May I put it in this wee book?

Jean: By all means.

RECOLLECTIONS FROM THE 'LAST HOUSE', BENSIDE, ISLE OF LEWIS

SEAN AND BEN STEPHEN were not born when their parents, BARBARA ZIEHM AND IAN STEPHEN first met Martyn and Margaret. Years later, Ian collaborated with Martyn on a few projects, including 'Snipe Shadow' on Hardland. The 'boys', now 18 and 20, have their own reminiscences of Martyn, while Barbara's first connection stretches back over more years. Though Ian is officially the writer (poet and storyteller) at 'The Last House', Barbara's email sparks off the memories:

Barbara: I first met Martyn and Margaret at the Highland Folk Festival in Dingwall. He must have been about 14. The two of them performed together—as well as playing his pipes, Martyn sang harmony on one of his mother's Gaelic songs—and I admired the strong relationship between mother and son. Some kids don't want to be seen dead with their mum at that age, let alone be on stage with them.

I had a suspicion that very day that I might be pregnant and ceremoniously had a last pint 'just in case'! I remember feeling at that point, "If this is true, and I am going to become a mother, I would like to have a rapport like these two." I was right, and my wish came true. My boys are now grown up and we get on well, even though we don't appear on stage together.

Martyn's music has always been around them. He managed to bring traditional music to young people in such an exciting, innovative way, constantly stretching the boundaries. The boys admire and love him for this, in particular where some of the pieces are a bit too 'wacky' for me; at times we have argued about the noise level ("Turn that b—— music down!"). Sean's dreadlocks and Ben's mixing desks can be both attributed to Martyn.

The last time we met at our house was when he recorded in Lewis. There was Kirsten, Martyn, Sean, Ben and me—my kids now older than Martyn was when I first met him. Does that make me a *cailleach* [old woman]? It was one of the funniest evenings I have ever had—the three boys sparking wit and wonderful conversation off each other, Kirsten and me making tea and things—quietly watching. It's a wonderful memory to have. Something I could never have foreseen or imagined, watching them, there on stage in Dingwall all those years ago...

Sean: I remember my dad coming back from working on the mainland and telling me and my wee brother about this crazy show he'd been to. And he handed over a CD—Bothy Culture. I listened to Martyn's voice counting to four on track 3, 'Sputnik in Glenshiel', and skipped back over and over and over again, just to hear those four words—that voice captivated me. Finally I'd let the tune run, dance round my room and think of nothing else. It's funny, now, maybe seven years later I still do that, skip it back and listen to the count, and it still triggers the same feelings. Ben was probably about ten at the time, and we were obsessed! 'Hallaig' was memorised, not on purpose, just through repeated listening.
"Who's Sorley Maclean, Dad?" I used to work on my Sorley accent, and we'd put on the CD when friends came over and be proud that we could recite it.

We went to see Martyn play in the town hall in Stornoway, and I must admit my memory of the music is hazy. I think the excitement and anticipation took over. What isn't hazy is the memory of Martyn in yellow waistcoat and tartan trousers,

'It's Not the Time You Have...'

swinging his crazy dreadlocks—man, talk about hero-worship! Wow! I'm surprised our first copy of Bothy Culture didn't wear through!

The second time I saw him play was in the big tent at the Hebridean Celtic festival on Lewis. Now, as an early secondary school pupil it was seriously uncool to be seen dead listening to that OLD music! If only they'd known—Martyn with full band pumping out the craziest tunes I had ever heard; we danced hard, and all night. Then the techno beats cut out and Martyn came to the front of the stage playing a perfect pibroch. I was captivated, totally and utterly hooked. Three in the morning and ears ringing we re-emerged from the sweaty tent, euphoric. I'd be willing to bet that we even listened to the CD in the car on the way home. Then came the struggle of trying to bring my friends round to the 'old' music, a few got it at the time, but now we all go to the Heb Celt Fest religiously every year. Everyone's got the bug, Afro Celt Sound System, Croft No. Five, the Peat Bog Faeries, to name but a few. Martyn is responsible for opening our eyes and ears to a wealth of tunes, of musicians, and of history and community, and therefore some of the best times of our lives. Look at the inlay card of Bothy Culture, under the CD—he hit the nail on the head.

Then, my dad told me about a phone-call from Margaret, saying that Martyn wasn't well—really not well. But after that Martyn still came to our house with Kirsten. No more crazy 'dreads' that I'd been fixated on, and clearly not well. But when he talked, the Martyn I'd known through his music was back. Everything he spoke about was passionate and exciting to listen to, he spoke openly about being ill and I felt privileged to experience that openness. It struck me that somebody who was going through what he was going through would have every right to be self-centred, or to give up, but Martyn seemed so interested and excited to hear what I had to say. I didn't feel like 'some teenager' when I talked to Martyn. I'll never forget that day at our kitchen table—or that night at the Heb Celt.

It goes without saying that Martyn's music is never off my CD player, oh, and guess what hairstyle I now have? (There's lots of them, and they're ginger!)

Ben: I got into Martyn's music through a copy of Bothy Culture. Dad brought it back after a trip where he had randomly recorded a crazy poem for 'Snipe Shadows', actually one of my favourite tracks on Hardland (I love the percussive laughs). I became immensely proud of this and me and my big bro started to spread the word about "this insane dreaded dude who plays the most wicked music in the world." The Scots Porage Oats advert made us go wild whenever it was on TV! I finally saw him in concert at the big tent during the Heb Celt. Easily the greatest performance I have ever seen! It brought me whole new genres of music as every year I have been back, now accompanied by my friends. We have become great lovers of modern traditional music, e.g., bands such as Shooglenifty, Croft No. Five, Jose Manuel and the Peatbog Faeries.

I have a couple of memories about 'Hallaig'—Sean and I used to have fun with that! I remember one time when Margaret was at our house, we were all sitting round the table—I was still in primary school and Sean was in the secondary, the Nicolson, in Stornoway. Anyway, we'd been listening to these adults going on about this and that, mostly about boats or some literary thing, as my Dad had been doing this writers' gig with Margaret—you know the way adults talk on and on after dinner. Anyway, at some point, let's say when they stopped to draw breath!—Sean and I suddenly started to recite 'Hallaig' in our Sorley MacLean accents. Mum and Dad grinned (cos they knew) and Margaret's eyes were wide open, and at the end she went, "Wow! I'm impressed! My old high school, the Nicolson, teaching you Sorley MacLean! That's fantastic! Fabulous!"

'It's Not the Time You Have...'

"Oh no," we said, "we got it off a Martyn Bennett CD," and I think we must have sounded like she might not know who he is, far less be 'some distant relative' as she used to tell us! We just love reciting that poem, but, the other thing is, Hallaig was the track my mum always hated! I think it was the eerie voice that did it, and so we had a clandestine thrill whenever she was out to blast it out at probably double the safety volume! Because of this, the words stuck in our heads naturally.

The few times I got to meet Martyn, I experienced good conversation, religious debate and of course the inspiring story of his illness—how he turned something as horrific as the loss of his amazing abilities into as complete and perfect an album as 'Grit'. He even gave us an early mix of this, which includes the original 'Liberation' cut—very different to the one on the album. Its just fantastic and a prized piece. Martyn and Kirsten signed my blackboard painted cupboard and he talked frankly to me about music (not like most adults treat 15 year olds). And in knowing a real life musician, his influence has made me take my own music playing into more than just a hobby but my entire life. Martyn was funny, honest and intelligent and I and many others (especially of my generation) consider him a genius.

When Sean and I were younger, we had 'Martyn Bennett Parties'—Margaret was amazed at that! My family once went to a party in Ullapool and some older teenagers (the hosts' son and friends) were bouncing about upstairs. Sean and myself were drawn into the fray. Since then we had a big all-night music jam at a friend's house. Halfway through, we moved the PA system into the living room and started blasting 'Hardland' out into Point[35] at 2 in the morning.

Other occurrences of random Martyn outbursts happened at Benside (of course) and even Ness as well as Stornoway itself.

'It's Not the Time You Have...'

Why does it have this effect? Probably because as well as being incredibly powerful and beautiful music, it's definitely very accessible for our generation. The fusion of folk (ingrained in our culture and day to day lives—radio station Isles FM every morning on the school bus) with dancy heavy beats (we get from the one night club 'The Heb' in town and the hard rock and even drum 'n' bass culture which we listen to every day) seems to turn a dull night into a mad party, especially played at volumes the louder the better. It is also music I listen to, to reflect, especially Bothy Culture and also 'Grit'. Music steeped with memories such as the day Martyn walked in on me drumming and offered a lot of great advice—and my sadness finding out about his illness, how serious it was and of course finding out he had died.

One of my best mates, Alex 'Alyth' Gilbert is just as into the music as me. It's constantly on his 'iPod' as he walks to and from our band practices. Soon after he really got into Martyn, the two of us were crashing round his room—'freaking out' as a deputy rector once remarked when we were going a little mental to 'Grit' in The Nicolson Institute's social area as opposed to studying. So there was Alex and me, with Hardland when Alex shouted, "Man we totally have to experience this live, lets do it! Wherever we have to go, even as far as Edinburgh," (end of the universe as far as I was concerned). I suddenly realized that Alex didn't know about the illness. Of course he was totally gutted—it was heartbreaking. We hugged quite long and hard for some spotty teenage guys and put on Bothy Culture where both of our Martyn memories began and we played it right through.

Love from Ben.

Nuair a theid na siuil bha na chu-radh ri cruinn.

A TRIP TO QUEBEC

TONY MACMANUS, guitarist, recorded in Glasgow, January 2006:

Tony: We played together frequently and very informally at various tables at festivals and pubs here and there. I think the first time was when Martyn was in Edinburgh, at the Tron. But I gradually became more and more aware of his music and the massive contribution he was making to new interpretations of Scottish music. His name was all over the Celtic Connections programme the first couple of years of this festival, and I was just embarking on my career, and I remember thinking—he was doing loads of his own sets and loads of support— and I'm looking at this programme thinking, "Well why don't you just give him his own festival, for God's sake!" And then finally I met him and instantly we were buddies.

It's kind of ironic that the one time that we actually played formally together, which you would remember very well, Margaret, was totally acoustic—in a church, in Gould, Quebec.[36] And we did some concerts with the three of us, you singing and both of us accompanying you, and some just the two of us, Martyn and me.

But it was a very important point in my life, because I was just embarking on this relationship, which has blossomed into a life commitment. Denise (now my wife) came from Halifax (Nova Scotia) and I came from Glasgow and on our first trip away together we met up in Montreal. I had been to Halifax a couple of times but this was first time she had travelled to meet up with me. And we had had many heavy conversations about spirituality and things like that, and we'd never reach an agreement—I'm a devout evangelical atheist, and Denise is NOT. And we were wrestling with this definition: How do you define spiritually? And the minute she met Martyn there was a big 'click' there. They kind of locked souls very quickly, and she said to me, "Now, there's a very spiritual person"—and who could disagree?

The festival in Gould was a great weekend, it really was, and I have very fond memories of it. We stayed in the same house as Martyn—you were in the other B & B—and Martyn, being the star, had been allocated the emperor sized bedroom, and with Denise being a kind of addition to the party, the two of us were in a small room. And he instantly, and very graciously, offered to swap.

We also have a lovely photograph that shall remain secret—taken at that B & B that did fantastic breakfasts—Martyn laughing, and modelling a very sexy red negligee that Denise had brought for the occasion—it's just such a sweet photograph! We were standing outside out on the patio and the weather was beautiful, and I don't know where this piece of apparatus came from, but Martyn decided to model it!

Margaret: The previous Quebec festival we were at was in Megantic, and we stayed in another wonderful B & B. And the landlord spilled his entire plate of dinner into Martyn's lap just before the gig. The poor guy was mortified but Martyn burst out laughing—at least he didn't get scalded. And he says, "Eh, you got a washing machine?" and the guy was just about crawling, "Oh, of course, of course!" So Martyn says to him, "Then don't worry! I'll tell you what, I'll bring down my two weeks washing and you can do the lot while you're at it. Now wasn't that just a great stroke of luck, spilling the dinner?" He was laughing away, and a look of relief came over this poor man's face!

'It's Not the Time You Have…'

Tony: I think Martyn had a great gift for putting people at their ease; people were very natural around him.

Margaret: When you played together at the Quebec concerts what was that like?

Tony: It was great! It was just beautiful, natural music-making—kind of stripping away all the stuff that Martyn was known for, all the beats and samples, electronic stuff. To me the essence of why Martyn was successful at what he did, is that he wasn't joy-riding with the tradition. His grasp on the raw tradition was very firm, and very honest, and there was a great deal of integrity about how he played straight traditional music—there are a lot of people out there who are joy-riding with the tradition, they don't really have a foot in it, and they're just using it to further their own thing. But Martyn was totally the opposite.

Margaret: Do you remember introducing the tunes and songs in French?

Tony: Yes, I remember the audience being very touched by this attempt on our parts to try and speak to them in their own language—it was a good thing to try and do.

Margaret: And you both joined in my choruses—

Tony: Absolutely! I remember the two of us doing the backing vocals in Gaelic—yes, and he wearing his Scotland shirt! It was just a lovely weekend!

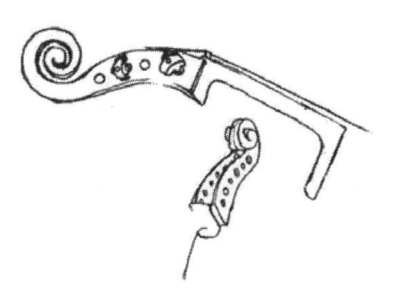

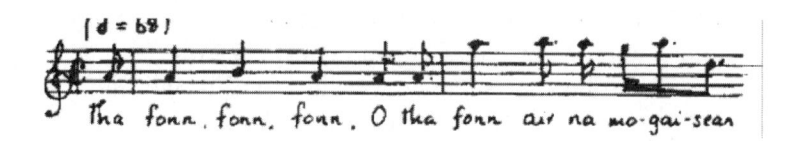

[♩ = 69]

Tha fonn, fonn, fonn, O tha fonn air na mo-gai-sean

MARTYN IN AMERICA

Although he had visited in early childhood, Martyn's first invitation to the USA came from singer and dulcimer player **LORRAINE HAMMOND**, Brookline, Massachusetts. Emailed from 'Great Acoustics'[37] January 2006:

Thinking about Martyn in America makes me smile hugely. I had the privilege of meeting Margaret in Edinburgh in 1986, met sixteen-year old Martyn in Scotland the following year, and in 1989 was able to book them both for Pinewoods Camp Folk Music Week in the States. It was Martyn's American debut. I wanted Margaret there for the transatlantic ballad connection and I wanted Martyn because he was a musical joy and delight—eloquent on his instruments and full of the kind of mad energy that enlivened a setting that can get a bit studious.

Martyn loved the rustic setting—the 'no cars', the basic cabins in the woods, the lake to swim in, the mix of all ages, the freedom—and the endless opportunities to play music. He even seemed to like his daily kitchen chores, wearing an apron and washing dishes! A sort of 'Will o' the wisp', he'd always do his own thing, find his own space, his own musicians. No use to ask Margaret where he was, unless they were scheduled to be together—then he'd appear. But when they made music or sang together, mother and son, the pair of them modelled a musical continuity that is rare and powerful.

And Martyn jammed with us all—bluesmen Silas Hubbard and Sparky Rucker, songwriters Gordon Bok and Bob Franke—shook up our perceptions and pushed musical boundaries, and just when he seemed dangerously close to the edge he pulled back with an exquisitely played set of Scottish traditional tunes on the pipes. It was a brilliant week.

The following summer we did it again, this time with three generations of the Bennett family—Margaret's mom Peigi agreed to come too. No matter that it was the wettest week of that summer, the jams pulled the whole camp together, and Peigi,

'It's Not the Time You Have...'

Margaret and Martyn offered a valuable insight into the passing on of musical tradition within family.

Mind you, my favorite Martyn musical memory that summer was coming upon a music lesson that Vermeer would have loved to paint! A rainy afternoon in a musty cottage by lamplight and guitarists Bob Franke and Bennett Hammond were patiently coaching Martyn who was struggling to erase note after note from his fiddle riffs until he could find and feel the deep guts of the blues.

Martyn always reached for the deep guts of music. He found it and he communicated it. Playing with Martyn was exciting. The experience was never trivial or shallow. Whatever our musical gifts were to Martyn, that was his great gift to us.

BENNETT HAMMOND, musician, Brookline, Mass.[38] Emailed from 'Great Acoustics' January 2006:

Do we have specific memory moments of Martyn's career development—or merely ones of our own awe and wonder? For one thing, we could never choose our favourite 'Martyn moment', since every meeting with Martyn, every conversation, every phone call was memorable and moving, exciting and instructive.

And as it happens, I do have an instance of his musical growth to cite, for I think I was there when Martyn 'got' the blues on the violin. Well, something happened, anyway. Bob Franke and I sat with Martyn one of the many rainy afternoons at Pinewoods, just playing 12-bar blues and getting him to slow down, down, showing him ways to keep it simple, like repeating a phrase through the chord changes without modulating it. That was probably the last time I knew anything that Martyn didn't, and he got it right away. He shot past me and Bob, way up the string beyond the fingerboard, soaring slurs and snotty slouching solos, but humbled by the simple insistence of the groove. He was 'gone'. Now, I dare say he knew how to do most of that before he came to America—but I'll bet I was the first teacher to encourage it!

SARAH BAUHAN, flute and whistle player, Boston. Emailed January 2006:

Our teachers come in many forms, ages, and sizes. One of my greatest was Martyn. He was 19 and I was 30. We were all at Pinewoods for a week that summer—I was asked by Lorraine at the last minute to come to fill in for someone, so it was by chance that I was there. I had lost my mother to a fight with alcoholism in February of that year, on, or within a day, of Martyn's birthday, as it happens.

After lunch one day, Martyn and I were in the open-sided dance pavilion 'noodling' around on stuff, trying out some tunes—he on the piano, me on the whistle. By and by, I played a lament that I had just written for my mother—I didn't say anything about it, just played. Listening intently, Martyn put some chords behind it as I played, and when we stopped, he turned around to me and said, "That was the most beautiful tune I've ever heard. What was it?" Embarrassed, I mumbled something about my mother. By this time the rain was coming down in sheets, all around us, but we huddled by the piano, Martyn with music manuscript paper, hands on the keys, pen in his teeth, working out, as only Martyn could do. Within a half an hour he had this most amazing, evocative arrangement of my simple melody.[39] It was one of the most intense two hours I have ever spent.

We decided that we would play it in the concert that night, but I said to him that I didn't want to tell people what it was. And we did. We played it, and as it ended I broke down and sobbed, those gut-wrenching sobs. Martyn came over and put his arm around me and said quietly into the microphone, "That was a lament that Sarah wrote for her mother who just died in February."

Over the next few days, people came up to me and told me that they too had been crying. They told of how they had lost someone near and dear, and they hadn't really felt it until that moment, and how grateful they were. Until that moment, when I experienced that absolute catharsis, with all those people present to bear witness to my grief, I had no clue how powerful was this gift of music that I had been so freely given. Martyn accessed that for me on that day, and, ever since then, I have been trying to give to others what I feel was his gift to me—for Martyn really did change my life.

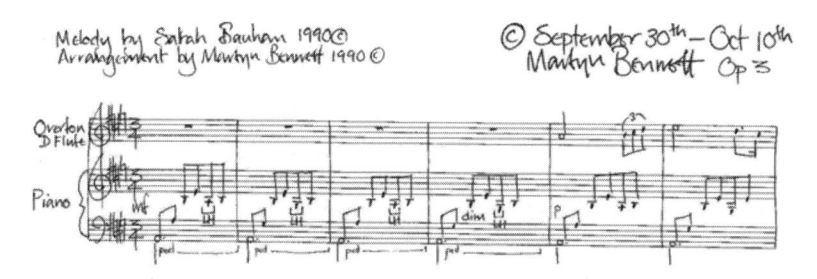

[Musical score: Melody by Sarah Bauhan 1990©, Arrangement by Martyn Bennett 1990©. © September 30th – Oct 10th Martyn Bennett Op 3. Overton D Flute and Piano parts.]

Later that year, I was fortunate to be able to head over to Scotland and record Martyn's piano arrangement of the lament for my mum. And then a couple of years later Martyn worked out and recorded another piece that I did for my second CD. There is a coda to all of this. On the second piece that he arranged—another lament as it turns out—Martyn had just gotten his first midi-synthesizer-thing. I'm embarrassed to say I don't know what it was called! He did the whole arrangement and programmed it all, and in fact he did three or four versions of this for me. Naturally he liked the wildest one—with big drums and lots of percussion. I remember his disappointment when I went for the tamest of the arrangements, because he was so excited about what he'd done, and he just wanted me to be sharing that excitement with him. I was still in that place where I hadn't gotten past my fear of what people would think. I then added my flute track back here in the

States and when the album came out, I too was very disappointed with my choice. Not just tame, but the flute sounded awful to me—it was very flat, both in pitch and in the performance. So, to do justice to Martyn's creativity and as a to tribute him, I have dug out the DAT tape with the 'big' arrangement and am putting it on my next CD that I am currently working on with a big low whistle that is in tune!

In addition to the earlier lessons learned from Martyn, sadly his death has also taught me so much—mostly about seizing the moment and not wasting it.

JOANIE BRONFFMAN AND NEAL MACMILLAN, Boston. Emailed January 2006:

We were at the same Pinewoods camps where we met Martyn—and the second one, when Lorraine brought him over, young as he was, he was among the teaching staff. Anyway, Neal, who plays small pipes and fiddle, took some piping lessons from him. Of course we not only kept in touch but loved him to the last.

Towards the end of his life, one time when Martyn called us on the telephone and we were talking about various things, he asked if we were still playing music. We said, "Yes."
He said, "Do you know 'Fingal's Cave'?" We said, "No."

He ran and grabbed a whistle to teach us the tune over the phone. We learned it immediately. We play it frequently as it always reminds us of our special friendship and musical exchanges.

JERRY EPSTEIN, former Music Director of the Christmas Revels, New York. Email, January 2006:

We brought Martyn to New York in December 1991, as one of the soloists in the 'Christmas Revels'—a week for rehearsals, then six shows at Symphony Space, Broadway.[40] I was the

'It's Not the Time You Have...'

musical director, and Martyn, a student at the RSAMD at the time, played Highland and bellows pipes, fiddle, and did some dance steps as part of the general banter.

I was always impressed with Martyn's piping — I assume I heard it first at Pinewoods. Some of it was quite untraditional, particularly the way he inserted cross rhythms (triples in common time, or quadruples in waltz or jig time), but all of it was so eminently musical. It didn't feel like showing off, but like a kind of high spirited playing, teasing, with the traditional form. Thus I was delighted when he and Margaret came to the US to join Norman Kennedy in the Christmas Revels New York production.

Twice during the show, Martyn played Highland pipes for the beautiful dancing of Karen Campbell and the way the two enjoyed each other was obvious. They developed a little routine where Karen had to put Martyn's shoes back on WHILE he was playing. . . the director left it in and didn't try to change it, even though it had nothing to do with the script. It was so damned much fun they were having, it was quite infectious. What I found most memorable looking back on it, was that same sense of playfulness, humor, teasing—Norman still laughs about it. Norman shared an apartment with Margaret and Martyn for the whole time, so he could not escape Martyn's clowning. That year we had a Celtic theme, Scottish Gaelic Hogmanay customs, some of which have died out. (Margaret and Norman both made huge contributions to the development of the script, including one bit – 'The Four Tradesmen' – which actually Martyn gave me. I think he did it as a kid with his cousins or something – brought down the house every time.)

At the last night party we saw that Martyn, who could sometimes appear a bit disconnected, had taken in all in—not just the tunes and songs, but the mannerisms of the stage manager, Gary Miller! When we were least expecting it, we heard Gary's voice: "'K-folk! That's enough! That's enough! C'mawn! Pay attention! C'mawn, c'mawn, now don't get me stahted!" Then, drawing his hand through his hair, Gary style, Martyn did this take-off, a mock serious Manx dirk dance—I won't tell you what he called it. Let's just say Margaret needed to look somewhere else!

In the later times I saw Martyn, and in the many things I heard about his busy life, it seemed to me like those days in the Revels were among his most fun. He seemed quite carefree, totally relaxed, enjoying what he was doing without pressure. I think it was not long after that that his cancer was first diagnosed—perhaps a couple of years—so I rather doubt that he could ever have been that carefree again. It was not an easy life. I can only hope that that time in New York was great for him. He contributed a great deal.

GLORIA M ROSSON,[41] Celtic Connections regular from California, sent this note while in Glasgow visiting Showcase Scotland, January 2006:

I first met Martyn when he agreed to play pipes for Woolfstone on their first US tour. Small in stature and mighty in talent, he elevated the level of musicianship at the gig, and he raised the musical consciousness of the thousands who saw him play, from California to Canada.

I can still see him, the mad imp in America, as he nearly passed out from lack of oxygen playing high in the Rockies at the Telluride Festival. He would step off stage for a moment, for oxygen, (provided by the festival) then return to play simply amazing pipe music. I can see him too, walking a thin wooden fence—like a tightrope through the Redwood Forests of Northern California—and I can hear his impish laughter as he struck out into the pitch black night (despite our warnings about bears) to find the thousands of frogs making amazing music in the Sierra Meadow near Yosemite after the Strawberry Festival.

There was always a beautiful simile on his face; and some impish mischief in his mind. But when he played—be it the Highland pipes, the whistle, or the fiddle—then there was magic.

I feel very lucky to have spent so many days with Martyn & co during that groundbreaking tour. And I know there are thousands of people in America who didn't know much about Scottish music, who became converts when they heard him play.

THE CAMERA AND THE MICROPHONE

TIMOTHY NEAT, artist, writer and film-maker. Emailed from Fife, January 2006:

> Look! Is that only the setting sun again?
> Or a piper comin from far away?

Last year I told Martyn that he will be one of those to whom I shall dedicate the biography of Hamish Henderson. (Presently I am engaged in writing, indeed almost finished the book, which will be published by Birlinn.) For some reason, Martyn seemed surprised.

Of all young people in Scotland, Martyn was the one who embodied Hamish's understanding of what the genius of Scotland is. He was the boy piper, the wild fiddler, the young Highlander; light-stepping, dreaming, like Donatello's 'David': he was youth bedecked in flowers—conjuring 'the ecstatic vortex of the dance'. He was the poetry that becomes people.

When I made the film 'Journey to a Kingdom' it was natural that Martyn should be the one to summon Hamish—with the pipes, with a Pan-ish nod—up to the North East: to leave Edinburgh and the School "an' com' awa' wi' me". And Hamish came to the great Jacobite window—called by the wind—and he looked out onto the Meadows to where Martyn was piping—with

'It's Not the Time You Have...'

Italian voices floating in the breeze—with the faces of Japanese girls breaking into smiles—with boys on bikes passing—with the archers competing for 'the silver arrow' and the music o' the pipes rippling through the leaves—drawing him 'again to our welcoming north'.

    A few years later, Martyn and Kirsten made the music for my Mary's wedding. Dressed in golden corduroy, he played beneath the ancient chestnut tree, at Balmerino— 'Mairi's Wedding', and that great pibroch-piece he'd just written. Their faces illumined against the darkness of the trunk and the shadow of the shade of the spreading branches: their music and their presence never to be forgotten.
Martyn, "There's nae hame can smoor the wiles o' ye," Man yer music poured forth like sunshine.

> [Your] duty done, I will try to follow you on the last day of the world,
> And I pray I may see you all standing shoulder to shoulder
> With Patrick Mòr MacCrimmon and Duncan Bàn MacCrimmon in the centre
> In the hollow at Boreraig or in front of Dunvegan Castle
> Or on the lip of the broken graves at Kilmuir Kirkyard,
> While, the living stricken ghastly in the eternal light
> And the rest of the dead all risen blue-faced from their graves
> (Though, the pipes to your hand, you will be once more
> Perfectly at ease, and as you were in your prime)
> All ever born crowd the islands and the West Coast of Scotland
> Which has standing room for them all, and the air curdled with angels,
> And everywhere that feeling seldom felt on the earth before
> Save in the hearts of parents or in youth untouched by tragedy
> That in its very search for personal experience often found
> A like impersonality and self-forgetfulness,

'It's Not the Time You Have...'

And you were playing: 'Farewell to Scotland, and the rest
   of the earth,'
The only fit music there can be for that day
And I will leap then and hide behind one of you,
A's caismeachd phiòb-mòra bras-shroiceadh am puirt.

Look! Is that only the setting sun again?
Or a piper coming from far away?

[From **Hugh MacDiarmid's** 'Lament for the Great Music']

July 15, 1997, a note from Hamish Henderson to Margaret (who was 'grounded' and had to miss the wedding):

Poor Margaret! I only wish that some alchemy could make those damnable problems vanish! Yesterday Kätzel and I were in Fife—in the grounds of the ruined Balmerino Abbey, to be precise... it was a great occasion! Martyn and Kirsten did splendid service—the composition was truly spine-tingling! Tim was wearing a kilt—MacLaren tartan! He looked magnificent.
See you soon, I hope.
    Love, Hamish.

SHEILA STEWART, Blairgowrie, Perthshire, singer on 'Grit', in conversation, January 2006:

Sheila: I've never met anybody yet that didnae like that track on 'Grit'—me singing 'Move', they tell it's the best they'd ever heard me! And a' the time people ask me, how long you've known Martyn? God, I knew his mother long before she ever had Martyn! I knew Martyn a' his life, and I was very, very close to Martyn—and his mum. And he was also very close to my mother, very much so. And one memory that I have o' my mother and Martyn is that my mother said that Martyn was the best young piper that she had ever heard. Now my mother

'It's Not the Time You Have…'

grew up wi' pipes, an' she knew a finger when she heard it—good, bad or indifferent, she'd tell you the truth, my mother. She wisnae a person tae mince her words! She could do the canntaireachd[42] like nobody else—'The Renfewshire Militia', and tunes like that—talk about timing! My mother wis jist steeped in piping—her father, and my own father. She was an amazing woman. There'll never be another Belle Stewart.

And of course, Martyn had such regard for her, because he composed for her, on her ninetieth birthday—'Belle's Fancy'.[43] He wrote it all out, and gie'd it tae her, and my mother was over the moon that a young boy would take the time to make up a tune for an old woman like her. It's a lively tune—my mother was a lively woman, though! Her character went into the tune, and I knew it would, because Martyn could see right deep intae my mother.

> My Dear Friend Margaret I recieved your very welcome letter …
> Theres nae freen like an auld freen and I don't mean in years…
> Cathie and Sheila and their families are all fine. and asking for you. now my young Boy friend I think he is a piper Na Na. give him a Big Hug and a Kiss for me I would like to ask a great favour of him could he ~~w~~ compose a march for me and call it Belle's fancy. I am maybe asking too much But I would realy love it it doesn't have to be a march any one will do god Bless you all take care guid folk are scarce
> all my love Belle.
> x x

There was a special bond between my mother and Martyn. It was unbelievable. Because Martyn was the type of boy, that, no matter what company he was in, he'd fit—if he was in young company, he could be young; if he was in old company he could be older; and there was never nae space of

'It's Not the Time You Have...'

age in between. And every time you think o' Martyn, you shouldnae think o' him through your head; you should think o' him through your heart.

Mind the first time she heard you singing 'Glen Lyon'? I think it was Muchty. And she said, "You've got the conyach. Do you know what that means? Oh," she said, "that song—it's a Perthshire song, of course." But I never heard anybody could sing it like you, Margaret—singin it fae your heart, you see, and it holds memories for you. And then Martyn grew up with it coming out of his pores so he was bound to feel it.

Now as far as the tradition goes—local or family—this is a big influence on musicians. And Martyn was a person that could concentrate on any type of music. No' just the 'funky' music—that's just one type of music, but Martyn was like unbelievable—like a musical dictionary. Martyn was a human dictionary that loved all types of music, though he grew up with the tradition. He just was a person that wanted to tap into all kinds of music, and he did it very, very successfully.

What's important is that he grew up hearing the tradition first, and the world music second—you could never, ever get any better than that. Growing up with the oral background that Martyn did—that moulded him into being a strong person to accept any type of music, but his first music was the tradition. And that was brilliant. Now there mebbe some who think that what Martyn got by folk's firesides wasn't really important, that he was just a bright music student and so he learnt it. But that's stupid folk, it's folk that disnae know what they're talking about! That's folk that wish they had it ingrained intae themselves, like Martyn had it ingrained into him. Mebbe a wee touch o' jealousy?

Martyn was always very at ease and natural wi' me, like we were family. Martyn felt like my son—it was unbelievable. When Martyn looked at me you saw his face relaxing. And I'll never forget the time Martyn got his first decks—that was in Edinburgh, and he was over the moon with this new decks, trying to find out how to use them. So me an' Cathy landed

'It's Not the Time You Have...'

there, and we stayed wi' you—was that no' the time that there was a concert at the Queen's Hall, and we were a' singing at it? And Ray [Fisher] wis there, we were a' there, stayed over, and the next day we were still having our breakfast at two in the afternoon. We never got away fae the table for talking an' singing!

Anyway, Martyn singled me oot and took me through to the room, and he was sitting wi' these earphones on, at the decks. "What do you think o' this?" he says, "my first attempt."

And he played me this thing, and I'm listening, and I says, "hold on a minute, Martyn—you're a wee bit too heavy-handed with the drums." So he toned down the drums, and then he says, "You go away now." So I went through, and then he come for me again, and I went back. "How does that sound?" he says, and I said, "That's perfect!"

Of course we'd meet at folk festivals dozens of times, but there wasn't a lot of young folk playing or singing then—now there's hundreds of fantastic young musicians, but in those days there'd be one or two youngsters, and that was it. But that was quality then; Martyn was quality. And he was the old-fashioned, the old way o' being brought up. And not very many youngsters, even in these days, had that thing behind them. You see, now everything's got to be done by music, precision, and things like that. Martyn had ten times more education in music than just book learnin. And he'd go everywhere—of course when you'd be out recording folklore, or when Hamish [Henderson] and you would go places, Martyn would be there, sitting listening. He was like an older person; he would fit in. You somehow didn't notice there was a child there.

And years ago, I mind being at your house in Kingussie—me and my Roy—he wis a few years older than Martyn. And Roy went outside to play wi' Martyn, and then afterwards Roy was singing, and Martyn, it was the pipes. And I mind the other person Martyn used to listen to was Willie MacPhee.

'It's Not the Time You Have...'

And see, Martyn and Willie together, they were always speaking about piping, you know—what makes a good piper. And mind one time at Muchty Festival[44], a nice, hot, sunny day and Jim Reid and the Foundry boys were playing and the big crowd around, and they had this wee boy, Martyn, playing with them. You should have seen Jim's face—just thrilled![45] And I remember Willie standing looking in, and he had that very intense expression he used to have, looking right at Martyn playing. And when they finished the tune he went right over to him and took those small hands in his huge big spades o' hands, and he says, "That's piper's fingers, laddie, that's piper's fingers." Willie was a lovely, lovely man, definitely. And you remember Willie MacPhee was one o' the first who actually encouraged him.

And Willie composed too—that tune, 'The Belles o' Loch Lochy', well my father made the first part when they were camped there, the four o' them— Willie's wife wis Belle too, Bella— and when they came back down from Loch Lochy Willie added another part tae it, for his Belle! And years later my Ian made a song for that first part, and Martyn transcribed the whole tune—it's in Tocher.[46]

I mind Martyn was so vexed when Belle and Willie got flooded out o' their caravan when the Tay burst its banks that January. Oh, it was terrible—I think they lost everything in

57

'It's Not the Time You Have...'

that flood—except Willie's pipes. And Martyn played at the 'benefit' at Balquhidder, he played his pipes to raise money for Willie and Belle. He just loved them.

Then after he left home, I mind the first time I met him as a man—in Edinburgh folk festival, at the Festival Club on Chambers Street. I walked in and he was sitting at a table wi' Cathal McConnel. And he saw me coming through the door, well, he near knocked me down [with a big hug]! And I sat for two hours talking to him sitting there, because I hadnae seen for a while. And I told him this was the first time I saw him grown up, but I said, "you'll aye be a wee laddie tae me, you know!" And we laughed!

Now when he picked me singing 'Go, Move, Shift' for 'Grit', he just surprised me. Well, he'd phoned me up one time, he said, "Sheila, would it be OK if I use your voice, because I've done 'Glen Lyon' wi' my mother's voice," an' he says, "would it be OK if I use your voice and bring it forward intae modern music?"

I says, "You do what you like wi my voice!"

And then, the first time I heard it was up in Inverness (when we were on the Scottish Women Tour) when you quietly asked John Weatherby on the mixing desk to play it, to put it on when we were clearing up after our show—made me sit in a big chair and put it on, wi a this sound round the hall! I thought you'd have had to call for an ambulance for me cos I'd never heard my voice like that! And Ray was there, going, "Wow! Sheila!" it was amazing, and that's the first time I heard it. That's right, that's right! Oh I approved very, very much! I just couldnae believe that my voice could come into modern music like that. And I loved the percussion. And Martyn's dream was that it should be heard all over the world. And then he wanted to put it on vinyl, just the one song, on vinyl. It was done in Germany and it was done in France, so that track could go round the clubs.

And then of course I went up tae Mull to do the second one, 'The Banks o' the Lea', when they were making that television programme. Well, they were both intertwined together—working with him in the studio, but when we were doing 'The Banks o' the Lea' I wasnae filmed, because Martyn didnae want any intrusion. So I just sat in his studio, in the hall, and he himself recorded me sitting at a table, singing 'the Banks o' the Lea'.

Now when we went away back home, to their house, beside him and Kirsten where I was biding, he stayed on, and he took what he had recorded up tae his studio. And then he took me up the next day tae hear it. And I says, "There's too much o' me in it. I want more percussion." Of course he burst oot laughin—it's on the TV documentary. Well, he said the company that made 'Grit' (Realworld) had said that there wisnae enough of my voice on it, so he says, "Sheila, you've got to sing the whole lot o' 'the Banks o' the Lea'. That's why," he says, "I have to make it you singin and I'll come in wi the percussion, the backing."

And I says, "As long as you go wooooOOOOF!"
You know, like he did wi 'Grit'!

Margaret: How did it feel to be there, working with him?

Sheila: Oh it was unbelievable! Just inspiring! Because I'd always seen Martyn in social settings but I never, ever was involved wi' Martyn in his work in the studio. And tae me that was an eye-opener, of the knowledge that Martyn had. And to tap into me, the way he did, as a great musician, we just blended in no problem. It was wonderful! He knew exactly what he was looking for and could bring the best out in you. It feels wonderful. He said to me, that wi' me being older than when we made the recording he used, he said, "I thought mebbe your voice had dropped, but Sheila you're singin that song better than you've ever sung it in your life, and you're still up there!" And I'm so, so sad that I never got a recording of that, to see how it turned out.

It was very exciting—oh aye, he wis in his element. "Even," he says, "just to have you here, Sheila, doing it live with me, that's ten times better than just hearing you on

'It's Not the Time You Have...'

record." That recording he used on 'Grit', 'The Stewarts of Blair' of course has been around for a while, in the house for years.

Working wi' Martyn, it's an experience I will never forget. It's deep intae my heart. He put me on a different scene altogether. You know, he tapped me into that—I'll never forget him for that. And yet, he was the same Martyn I always knew. He just used his knowledge.

It was great, just the two of us there, because we knew each other well. But if anybody else haduv been there it would have interfered wi' the bond that we had between us. I was relaxed, he was relaxed, and it wouldnae hae been the same if anybody else haduv been there. We laughed a lot! Because he never thought that an old woman from the oral tradition, that she could come in and change intae his way, at that particular time and say, "there's no' enough percussion!" I could adapt and he adapted. Martyn just laughed with delight. And he had this special way o' drawing out what he wanted, without dictating. Martyn never dictated. He just in his own nice quiet voice he would tell you. He wouldnae say, "You've GOT to do this." He would suggest, and then of course, wi' him suggesting, being Martyn, you did everything he told you to do! You'd be stupid not to! You just knew—but he didnae do it with stern authority, no. And you just knew he knows what he's talking about so I better do it. I never questioned him—you'd be mad to stand and argue. Oh you couldnae, because you knew he was right, then when you heard what he had done! Oh my God! It's unbelievable.

Did I contribute to his life? I'd like to think so—I hope so, and I'd like to think so, even if it was just friendship. Yes, there was a bond, stronger than I can tell you. What me and Martyn had together wisnae friendship. Friendship's too light a word to call it. It was a bond, but a bond of outstanding depth. He would bare his soul—oh, yes, he did, lots of times. He would tell me lots o' secrets he wouldnae tell anybody else, because he knew it wouldnae go any further. And he knew that

'It's Not the Time You Have...'

I would give him guidance wi'oot just sympathising wi' him, although I did sympathise with him. He told me lots and lots of things I would NEVER repeat, because that was between him and me and nobody else. Complete trust in each other.

Margaret: Sheila, tell me about your new book—

Sheila: Well, it's not about my own life, it's about the culture of the travelling people of Perthshire—my family's culture. There's songs, ballads, stories, recipes, riddles, jokes, there's a' the Cant language, and it'll be out this year. And Hamish Henderson said that our Cant language was the oldest in Scotland. The book that's coming out this year, it's being published by Birlinn in Edinburgh. And I know who'd have loved that book—Martyn. But he's not far away, nor ever is.

A letter from folklorist Hamish Henderson (1919—2002), written after Martyn visited him with a recording of an early version of tracks on 'Grit'. (As far as we know, this is the last letter Hamish ever wrote, as he died less just over two months later):

19 Dec. 2001
Dear Martyn,
I am delighted to hear about your new music. Brave new music!! Davie Stewart would be proud to know his voice will be heard the world over. I give you my blessing to use my recordings.
     Love, Hamish.

FLORA MACNEIL, Isle of Barra and Glasgow, singer on 'Grit', in conversation, January 2006:

Flora: I enjoyed 'Grit' so much! And I said that to him, "You know, I enjoyed that CD from the start, from Sheila giving it her all, her heart and soul, to the very quiet one at the end, the story."

Margaret: How did you feel about what he did on 'Grit' with your song, 'Mo Rùn Geal Òg'?
Flora: It was fantastic, really! It was wonderful what he did—he worked wonders with the music.
Margaret: How did this come about—did he ask your permission?
Flora: He phoned me and mentioned it, and I said, "Yes, of course you can," and he said "Oh, I'll have to get permission from, you know—" And I said, "don't bother!" But you know one has to do that, and he would do everything right—he would, and he did, you know. Oh, he was wonderful, he just understood the whole scene, really… I remember years ago, one time up at the Moray Firth, we did a recording, a television thing—we were singing and he was playing. And in the hotel, wherever we were staying, I sang '*Fhir a Leadan Thlath*', and I'll always remember, he came over, and he said, "Oh Flora, that's your song! That's your song!" And you know, he was quite emotional—now I always remember that.[47] In fact I was getting to know him then. He was very natural and at ease, very much so. And he was such a musician, he could just play anything— pipes, anything! And of course '*Mo Rùn Geal Òg*'—he just loved that one. He seemed to understand songs—and he wanted people to hear those voices, that was his attitude. He came to the Scottish Women Concert in Edinburgh, the night I was singing—I sang 'Mo Rùn Geal Òg' and I said that I was singing for him that night. Oh, he enjoyed that! And I think the last time I saw him was at Celtic Connections, at the Royal Concert Hall, with Kirsten. And the next time I sang '*Mo Rùn Geal Òg*' was at his memorial concert—it's a way of expressing what you feel, it's difficult to explain, but it's easy to sing. And singing for Martyn that night, at his memorial concert I felt, "Right, he must be here!" I admired him so much, a wonderful, wonderful boy—I always think of him as a boy [laughs], but he was so young, far too young to leave us.

'It's Not the Time You Have...'

VARIATIONS ON A THEME

In October 2004, the National Mod in Perth opened with a special concert of a Gaelic version of 'MacKay's Memoirs'. Performed by the City of Edinburgh Music School, the event not only celebrated the richness of Gaelic song, music and language in Scotland but also around the world. Martyn was not well enough to attend the actual concert, but, a few weeks before the Mod, he recorded the resonant voice of internationally renowned Gaelic scholar Dr John MacInnes reading the Gaelic psalm. A seasoned broadcaster, lecturer and public speaker, John has known and our family since he recorded Peigi (Martyn's grandmother) in the 1950s. Having known Martyn since he arrived in Edinburgh as a youngster, John had also discussed many aspects of tradition with him over the years. Working with Martyn was, however, another matter, for despite having had fifty years experience in recording studios, the session in Martyn's make-shift home studio left a lasting impression on John. First of all, however, John tells of his connection to Martyn:

JOHN MACINNES, recorded in Edinburgh, February 5, 2005:

John: My association with this family goes back a long way—half my family come from the Isle of Skye. And I met Peigi, Margaret's mother, Martyn's grandmother, in 1953… Around 1984, I remember Martyn and myself, travelling up to the Isle of Skye, (with his mother), and I, being an old man, was sat in the front and Martyn, in the back seat, had a penny whistle. Of course there were discussions on all manner of topics, points of landscape and so on, then, during a lull in those conversations Martyn started playing this penny whistle, transposing a difficult piobearachd, [taught to him by David Taylor in Kingussie]. He transposed the entire piobearachd onto the penny whistle, and it was really quite extraordinary. I'll never forget it as long as I live...

And that extraordinary gift—and gifts—that Martyn had, continued to develop and proliferate until, when his time came, he had done so very much, so much that would make his fame enduring. I'm going to say a word or two in Gaelic which is the native language of this family—*Sìth do Mhartainn Dhonn a' Bhealaich*. And I translate that line, "Peace to Brown-haired Martin of Beallach". The Martins of Beallach in Skye were a noted family.

Peigi: We are actually related to them—we are descendents of them.[48]

John: Yes, I know that—to the noble Martins of Beallach in Skye.

JOHN MACINNES, from his letter, February 1, 2005:

As you probably know, he phoned me in the winter and asked me to record the 121st Psalm in the Gaelic prose version. I was so impressed by the meticulous concern he brought to the work—making me do it time and again, with specific directions, until he said, "That's it!" What it cost him in expenditure of energy I cannot imagine, but actually he showed no sign of weariness, and we talked for a long time afterwards. Martyn was buoyant and cheerful all through the evening. Such a magnificent spirit makes one very humble. Few people indeed could have mustered such spiritual, emotional and in fact physical powers in his condition. In my own experience he was unique in that regard. Bur he was unique also, as so many have testified, in his gift as a composer... I am morally certain that his work will be celebrated formally and informally in time to be.

Sìth do Mhartainn Dhonn a' Bhealaich

'It's Not the Time You Have...'

HAMISH NAPIER, Grantown-on-Spey—'Back of the Moon'[49]—recorded in Glasgow, January, 2006:

Hamish: I was still in school when I got into the recording studio with Martyn. Basically you phoned me up, Margaret, and asked would I like to do some songs, cos Findlay was doing some songs on the album, 'In the Sunny Long Ago'. An album with Martyn! I was already a total fan—I had the CD 'Bothy Culture'—just fantastic, so I was really excited about it. Before we went to Mull, we had a few rehearsals for it, we worked on it, and had what we thought was really set in stone—about three or four rehearsals and stuff, and it was all sorted. And I was really happy with my harmonies, cos I was just getting into vocal harmonies and starting to learn harmony on piano. And we went in to Tobermory, to his studio (at An Tobar)—remember the night before we practised the songs? Sitting in the B & B, saying, "This is good! Wait till Martyn hears this!"

And then we went in, and it was like, [laughs]—he was not impressed by it, or the harmonies that I'd come up with. Because what I'd come up with was, to him, really obvious harmonies and that. They sounded good enough, and we had no problem with them. I think what he said was, "Well, you could, eh... well, now, let's start again." Actually, to be honest, do remember feeling really cross. Of course, being young, this is being really cocky, you know—but I actually remember being really, really cross, thinking it sounded really, really good. But he stripped it right back, and the way he went through this harmony, just for that song, 'An t-oir òg', and then he took the harmonies apart again, and he sang this bass line, which was brilliant. He took it, and straight off the spot he chose harmonies for all of us. And if ever you missed your own harmony he went back to you instantly—he'd drop his own line, pick up your note and sing it with you just to get your one sorted. And he built it up, and just constructed a whole new harmony for everybody. He had a big picture of the

'It's Not the Time You Have...'

whole thing in his mind, and first of all I thought they were more boring, but when I heard them all together, it was like, these are totally amazing! Totally brilliant, and I just remember that's when I suddenly realised that I totally and utterly trusted him, although he'd been like, "nah, never mind this," what he then came up with, it blew me away! I realised that I could totally trust this guy one hundred percent as a producer, cos [laughs] I realised how much I had to learn. He seemed to put everything into it. When he taught you your part, he'd be looking at you, like there was nobody else in the world, straight at you, in front of your face, he'd have this hand beating— eyes popping out of his head, looking right at me! [laughs]

First of all you thought it was like, perfectionist, but it wasn't really that—he just wanted to get it right. That's one of things he taught me: if you've got an idea you might as well get it absolutely right. It's only going to take you ten, fifteen minutes, but you get it absolutely right. The attention to detail is really important—it doesn't take away the soul of the music. People sometimes complain about things being out of tune, things being slightly rhythmically out, and folk go, "Oh, that's just gives it the sort of, the authentic feel." But I don't actually believe that, and that's one of the things Martyn taught me. He tidied it up and got everything else perfect, it still sounded authentic—it was in tune, it was in time. I realised it was the standards that he had—probably his classical training that sort of came through?

Margaret: Well, you're asking me—but I think Kirsten would tell you, he was like that with everything. He'd say, if something is worth doing, it's worth doing well—carpentry, gardening, whatever, he was the same with everything— what's the point in doing it if you're going to it half-heartedly? When it came to recording, nothing was too much trouble. He seemed tireless— I have a photograph of you lying on the floor of An Tobar—you're only 18 and you're desperate to sleep and he's still going, "OK folks, five minutes"!

'It's Not the Time You Have...'

Hamish: We went to Mull do the gig live, so we did a concert in An Tobar with a lovely audience. Martyn recorded it (you really wanted the audience joining in the choruses), and some of it was good. Then he said, basically, we'll just stay and we'll actually record it again, ourselves.

Remember when we came with the album we had half Gaelic and half Scots, a bit of a hybrid, and what he decided to do was to have a theme, a whole feeling, sort of like a movie setting for the album. So he tried to create that atmosphere, and he set it up for us. Next thing he's carrying in this beautiful Indian carpet, 12 by 12 pink carpet, so he had us, like, all sitting around the fire in the evening, and with creaky chairs— he actually got out the creakiest chairs he could find, cos he didn't mind the fact that the chairs creaked cos that added to the whole thing! He even dug out a standard lamp, so he set us up with this standard lamp on that big rug, and chairs all facing each other.

Next day we were recording—playing from ten in the morning right up till three the next morning. And it was just a beautiful atmosphere that night, you know. We'd be going for the third or fourth take, or something, and it was still just totally beautiful. A lovely atmosphere, all the lights were dimmed, except for this standard lamp, and us all singing these songs.

And his studio was up a flight of stairs above this room— with a window looking onto it— and he must have run up and down these stairs dozens of times. It was like, "Hang on!" then, doo-doo-doo-doo-doo-doo-doo-doo-doo-doo-doo- doo-doo—him running up those stairs! [laughs] Energy for all of us, just fantastic! Totally fantastic!

Actually the other thing that amazed me as well, I knew that he was a brilliant classical pianist, violinist, viola player, percussion player, the whole lot, and it was no bother with the mixing desk—I always remember watching the mixing desk, and him totally working away at it, at lightening speed. Actually, I've never seen anybody do it that fast, hands going totally fast, amazing. But the thing that got me—it's quite mad—was his whistle playing! You don't get many whistle players like this. And there's not many Scottish whistle players but he's got to be right up there in the top ten ever. What he played was totally simple, hardly any ornamentation, but just a clear, pure, beautiful tone out of the whistle. And all he had on that night was an average whistle, but he was just able to produce a beautiful tone. And on 'The Rocks o' Merasheen' he had a big solo at the end of it, and we did all the different takes, it was different every time. The solos were amazing and the tone was beautiful.

And you'd asked me to play some accordion in the album, and I was just into learning all those grace notes. But he thought it would be like nicer if I didn't try and make it more fancy. It wasn't that he thought I couldn't do that—he thought it would actually be better if I just kept it totally simple.

And I remember Gillian [Frame] also had a few things— teaching her a few bits and bobs as we were going along, talking to her about how she could do this or that, showing her. So we learned loads.

Margaret: Yes, I remember him taking Gillian by herself and showing her some techniques. But he took us all by ourselves, including me—I remember your face, and Findlay's! You just looked at one another when he would correct me just like anybody else!

Hamish: Yes, and we're going, "I can't believe it!" I couldn't talk to my mother like that, telling her what to do! I seem to remember he was like, "Mum, that's naff! That's cheesy, that's—" You know, saying you can't do that, you ought not to do that, it was so to the point! But I thought you took it, you just went, "Right, OK, we'll try that," cos you trusted him as a producer one hundred percent cos you knew, like, I think everybody goes through that thing—when he cancelled all those harmonies we'd arranged, and came back with new ones

'It's Not the Time You Have...'

a million times better, that's when I realised, I'll just do exactly as I'm told!

Margaret: You and Findlay seemed surprised I didn't react, but that's easy, cos I didn't feel like reacting. I was probably the only one that was not really surprised—and it wasn't as if I was hiding it! [laughs] No, I never felt annoyed; I was absolutely fine being corrected by him. I was used to it because we'd done so many gigs together over the years—and he had actually recorded me for 'Glen Lyon' by that time.

Hamish: And it was because we did that album we got 'Back of the Moon' together, after that. And in fact, Gillian and I worked together, and it was only about a couple of months later that Simon McKerrell and Gillian and I got together and 'Back of the Moon' started. So that was a good sort of training to get in before Back of the Moon.

A NOTE FROM MARGARET TO FINDLAY, GILLIAN AND HAMISH, March, 2000:

At last! I've been holding off writing till I got the CD masters from Martyn—have a listen, let us know what you think.

First of all, thank you so much for sharing this with us—it was great fun—at least from my point of view. I have no doubt we all learned a lot too. (Not the least, me—I always rediscover how little I know!)

Also pretty special was the discovery that we could all go away together, travel, share space, meals, time, songs, ideas and, in such intense and concentrated efforts, still laugh together all the way through. Maybe that was best of all, and bodes well for all of us.

I'm off to North Carolina till April 26 so hope we can all share ideas after that. We'd like to get this out as soon as possible—any ideas on that too? I think youse all sound great—just wish you'd done something about your singer!

'It's Not the Time You Have...'

Meanwhile, I hope all is going well for you. We'll catch up soon! Aw the best, aw the time, and keep singing!
Love, Mgt.

P.S. I made some NOTES, jotted down after the recording sessions in Mull:

Been playing around with some ideas for an album title—maybe 'The Mull Sessions'?
'From the kitchen to the hall....' is another possibility?
Only, after our plan to use the recording he made of the concert in An Tobar, Martyn had us revert to the informal setting.
Probably going to be 'In the Sunny Long Ago'—the last line of 'Pat Murphy's Meadow'. That's one of songs I hadn't sung for years but Martyn insisted, "you must remember it!" He remembered it from heaven knows when, because we left Newfoundland when he was four! Anyway, I woke up in the next morning with the words in my head—maybe I didn't sleep! (Actually, I missed out a verse—don't tell!) Meanwhile, I've done some album notes—I'll run them past Martyn—no doubt I'll have to cut them[50], but this is a start.

DRAFT FOR MARTYN:

Most of my songs were learned in kitchens—to begin with, at home in Skye, then Lewis, then Shetland, and from the age of 19, Newfoundland, where I was just as much at home. After ten years (the last one in Quebec), back to Scotland again, this time in the company of my best friend, Martyn, who was about to turn six. We loved singing together, at home, in the car, anywhere, and he had already made his debut at a village-hall concert reported in the local newspaper who snapped 'the four year-old step-dancing to the lively accordion music of his friend, Gordon, aged seven who had taught him the tunes and the steps.' In these days, every Friday and Saturday night, or any other night besides, a crowd of us would gather in someone's kitchen for what every Newfoundlander calls a 'kitchen time'. And 'time' has nothing whatsoever to do with the clock. If it was your turn to sing, you'd do one of the old favourites and we'd all join in, song after song, hour after hour. Inevitably you'd pick up new songs, and though they all started off in the kitchen at some time or other, most of them made their way to the village or town hall or even to the concert hall.

This session, recorded over two visits to Mull, March and September 2000, remembers some of our favourites, so naturally there are a few from Newfoundland. Somehow the late nights seem much later to me than they once were, but the new generation that sings the songs has every bit as much enthusiasm for those kitchen sessions as ever I remember. Gillian, Findlay, Hamish and Martyn all grew up in families where singing was as natural as breathing — may they never run out of breath.[51]

'GLEN LYON' IN TRANSITION

The extract that follows was written the day after Martyn recorded the songs that eventually became his album 'Glen Lyon'. The recordings were made over a year before he suggested doing the 'In the Sunny Long Ago' album—more than three years went by before his 'Glen Lyon' CD was released. The background was simply that Martyn told me he'd like to record me—he put it to me, along the lines of, "OK, you're not getting any younger, and you spend a lot of time recording other folk and forget that someone should record you!" At the time, he had the use of a studio in Pathways, the Church of Scotland premises in Edinburgh—"they're lovely people, and they're really interested in my stuff". So he set a date: "Be there at… No, bring your own car, I'll be there anyway..." There was no working title at that point, no plans that he spoke of, no suggestions as to CD label—simply "let's record. Just you write me a list of all the Gaelic songs and I'll choose." And that was how we began.

NOTES FROM THE STUDIO, written the day after a studio session with Martyn, December 1998:

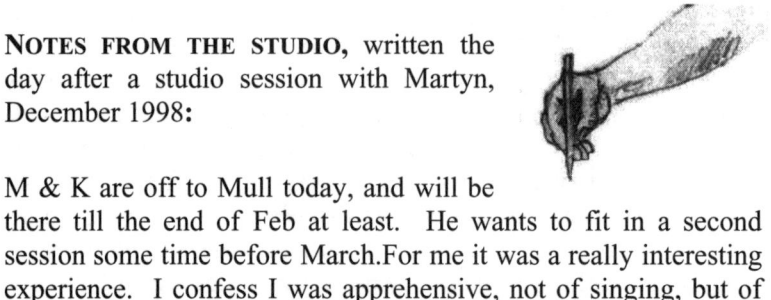

M & K are off to Mull today, and will be there till the end of Feb at least. He wants to fit in a second session some time before March. For me it was a really interesting experience. I confess I was apprehensive, not of singing, but of anything generating tension in his already tense life. And I can't but think, 'Record your mother, for goodness sake!'

After I made my list, I figured I'd better check the words of them with my own mother—she taught me most of them, after all. So, I do that, and she tells me, "Now Margaret, there are a couple of words in 'Griogal Cridhe' [the Glen Lyon Lament] that you keep changing—I'll write them out for you, so you have no excuse! And keep that paper in front of you when you record it—you have to get it right!" So, away I go, (thinking, funny how I seem to get instructions from all generations!)

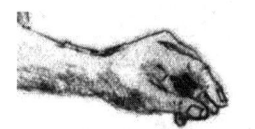

And here's a glimpse of what it was like—just notes, scribbled down after the session before I'd forget:

Martyn was so totally professional, patient beyond all my expectations—and every bit as demanding as I expected. Maybe more so. I can now understand better what Kirsten meant, when, after her first rehearsal of the band, Cuillin, she told me, "He's so demanding—and knows exactly what he wants and how to get it."

'It's Not the Time You Have...'

She's absolutely right, and she has 'way more experience of this than I do.

In the studio he tells me *he'll* choose the songs from the list—"this basically a list of my lifetime of your singing," he says.
"But where's *'Oran nam Mogaisean'* [the Mocassin Song]?"
And I say, "you're joking! I hardly every have a chance to sing it—it's not exactly what I'd choose to sing…"
"Who's choosing? Sing it anyway."
So, I say goodbye to the list, he keeps it, and goes down them one by one, picking out the Yes's and the Maybe's and the Definitely-not's, briefly giving his thoughts on each one.
And so we begin—he fixes the microphone for me in the studio, tells me exactly where to stand, then nips back behind the glass window (or is it a glass wall?) to his mixing desk, and puts on head-phones. He's already told me to pay attention and watch for the signals, and so we begin. I sing—he's looking straight at me. The hand waves, the face is serious, the eyes intense and alive with changing expressions. As soon as I see the signal to STOP, I do so. But he stops me frequently—for whatever reason, including (he tells me), 'lack of performance' (too tame ... that's not the way you sing it to an audience), bad timing (not again!), off pitch (will you please listen!), phrasing and interpretation. Now this really surprises me, interpretation, especially when sometimes he'd come out, and actually *sing* the song to demonstrate to me what he means. (Didn't realise how well he knew them, words to boot.)
And on it goes, till we come to 'Glen Lyon'.
"Music stand? What for?"
"Granny said…" and I tell him. So he goes along with this, not a word, gets the stand, I put the paper on it, and soon the signal to start. And the eyes are intense.
I'm not finished a verse when the hand waves 'Stop!'
I do, we start again—and again. This goes on several times, till, out he comes from the glass place, and, without as much as a glance at me, marches straight over to the music stand, snatches the paper, tears it up, smiles, and chucks the paper in the bin.

'It's Not the Time You Have...'

"Now SING!" says he, standing about a foot in front of my face, eyes wide, arms sweeping the air front of me.

"I can hear that blessed paper through the microphone!"

"But I never laid a finger on it," says she who knows perfectly well the sound of rustling paper through microphone. "Granny said—"

"Granny nothing! She's got nothing to do with this! It's not the paper I hear—it's your *eyes* on it! When do you ever sing with a paper in front of you? I can hear you looking at it! Do you get that? Now, sing—like you always sing it—WITHOUT that paper!"

I burst out laughing—I can't help it—not so much that it's funny, but it's like someone shone a bright light into a dark place in my mind.

"You know, that's absolutely true! I just never thought of it that way—you *can* hear my eyes!" He grinned, almost modestly and darted back into his glass-house (as I was calling it by then).

'Glen Lyon' again, this time with my thoughts on the meaning, on Gregor MacGregor, on his wife, her feelings, sorrow, heartbreak...

Song finished, Martyn said, "OK, next song."

Every song got a different reaction—and from his responses to them he clearly understood songs from the inside out. I had never given this a thought till we were in the studio—this must be my first real insight into Martyn's commitment to song, for I had never really seen this close up.

Visually, ever-changing, sometimes sitting with eyes closed, conducting the song, at times very delicately, other times wildly— passionate, fists clenched, but always in touch with the song in a way I had not really appreciated. Total focus—that's the way he is. And the amazing thing is that he never once 'tutted' (though he could have had plenty of reason). And he never once lost patience with me, or any enthusiasm, start to finish.

My comment to my own mother—after she had a laugh about the paper— was that I learned more about singing from Martyn in two days than from anyone else in the previous two decades. It was exhilarating. I'm writing this down now because it's an experience I must never forget.

      Best of all, we laughed a lot. At one point I was sitting on the floor, helpless, and now (darn it!) I can't remember what he said or did that had me in stitches, and him with the wry grin, laughing at me laughing. He tells me, "Mum, did you know your face looks like a hamster when you laugh?" which makes me laugh all the more, and he says, "See what I mean!" Two days in the studio and didn't fall out once. Whatever he does with this, he'll do. Meanwhile my 'homework', he tells me—write the words, notes. Think about an album title. We'll talk in a few weeks... Don't call me, I'll call you...

Postscripts (there seem to be several):
Title? I suggested *'Buan'* [Harvest]—"No, it doesn't look good and people will mispronounce it. And no, you can't write 'boo-an', that's naff. Have to think about this some more... not sure about this; still working on it—not sure it's your album yet..."
In the meantime, a year later, and still can't decide, he tells me "let's record some of the other stuff, like all those songs we all used to sing at home..." And so, I asked Findlay [Napier]—and thus we made 'In the Sunny Long Ago', which came out two years before 'Glen Lyon'.[52]

Reflections on the song, *'Griogal Cridhe'*, The Glen Lyon Lament:

This Perthshire song dates to the mid-1500. A family favourite taught to me by my mother, it was also a favourite of Hamish Henderson's (my former colleague and very dear friend). Hamish's roots are in Perthshire, and over the years I sang it for him many times, almost always at his request—at festivals, ceilidhs, and celebrations such as his 70th, 75th and 80th birthdays, and Martyn was at a good few.
When Hamish died on March 8, 2002, his family asked me to sing at his funeral in St. Mary's Cathedral, Edinburgh, on March 15.

There was really only one song I could sing for Hamish—his beloved 'Glen Lyon Lament'.

April, 15, 2005
Finally, the most poignant occasion of all, Kirsten invited me to sing 'Glen Lyon' at the memorial concert for Martyn at the Queen's Hall on April 14. Knowing how much Martyn loved this song he knew from earliest childhood, and contemplating on how he played the fiddle so beautifully for our recording— literally weeping with my singing—it seemed the only song I could sing for him. Words cannot convey our pain of losing such a 'sweet fragrant apple'[53]— or the physical pain of singing about such a loss. I now must sing it as we first heard it within the family— unaccompanied—for no musician I have ever met could accompany the song as Martyn did. He knew it from the inside, having walked with Kirsten every step of Glen Lyon. Before mixing the track, he sat on the top of the mountain overlooking the glen just to experience the song as close to its source as humanly possible. For Martyn nothing was too much effort when it came to understanding songs and music — he gave his whole heart.

JOHN AND MISHA SOMERVILLE, Croft No. Five[54] musicians, Ardbriachan, Inverness-shire, in conversation, Glasgow, January 2006:

John: Martyn had a big influence on our music—I mean I couldn't really underestimate Martyn's influence. I think the first time I certainly saw Martyn was when he was on TV, I think it was a show on BBC Scotland a while ago.
Misha: It was the Celtic Connections programme—they filmed Martyn in the Fruitmarket.
John: Yes, and we must have been about fifteen, sixteen, something like that at the time. We were sitting watching this Celtic Connections programme, and all of a sudden, there was

this dreadlocked guy playing on stage, playing dance music, you know, sort of modern urban kind of music mixed with pipes and whistles. And of course we both played a bit of music at that time, but we'd never really seen anything like that before! And it just captivated us, all of a sudden to see this guy there, doing this. And I think ever since that point, I've always been a massive fan of Martyn. I would confess to say that, along with the other band members we're probably his biggest fans—we followed him everywhere! We used to go to, I don't know how many gigs where he was playing, from Lorient in France, we saw him at the Lemon Tree in Aberdeen, and up at Cairngorm which—there's a nice story about that, actually! Up at Cairngorm and all over the Highlands—Tobermory… We used to have a camper van, didn't we? [laughter] Misha drove—I wasn't insured. When Misha turned eighteen my parents bought a camper van and it was great, cos we could take about seven or eight people in it quite comfortably. And we used to kind of tour around in this van, didn't we?

Misha: Often we'd be playing in places as well.

John: Well, I play the accordion, that's my main instrument—

Misha: And I play the whistles.

John: And I think in high school we used to sit in the practice rooms—you know these wee rooms in Charleston Academy in Inverness, and we'd sit there and we'd put this music on because we were the Martyn Bennett fan club! And we'd put it on, and friends would sort of drift in and out of the practice rooms where this music was, and these were people who wouldn't ever consider sitting down and listening to that kind of thing. And my friends would come in and go, "What's that you're playing?" And we say, "That's Martyn Bennett," and there was a real kind of pride in saying that you knew this music! It was like you felt quite special that you'd discovered this, and for that reason, we made it our intent to try and go to as many Martyn Bennett shows as we could. We sort of followed him everywhere! And obviously we played in a band as well, and that was a big influence to see someone young, out there, really making it. Having the sort of confidence to go out, by himself, at the start, before Cuillin Music formed—he was by himself for quite a long time and then Cuillin Music came about. You know the influence that had—to give us the confidence to try and go out, as a band ourselves, and say, "we want to try and do this full-time!" It was immense.

At that time we had a bass player, Sorley MacDonald. His dad, Donnie, was the maths teacher in Kingussie, so there was a bit of a connection there. Sorley always used to like that, you know, the connection between himself and Martyn which was great, cos Sorley was quite a passionate kind of a guy—about Scotland, and Scottish roots, and that, so it was a great thing that he knew Martyn in that way. And Barrie Reid who was playing guitar, he was part of the fan club as well. I mean we all stayed in the Inverness area. We'd all get together and go to these places together. And then Paul Jennings who, at the time, probably was doing a bit of touring with the Old Blind Dogs—he used to play with them, percussion. So, there was quite a squad of us. And Adam [Sutherland] joined—now, one of the things Adam always says, he never actually saw Martyn play a live gig, and that was one of the things that he really missed. He never saw the whole kind of, from the start through the Bothy Culture album and Hardland. He didn't ever really see Martyn playing any of that. So he kind of regrets not seeing that — but he still obviously—well, we all eventually met him. [And Adam played at the Martyn Bennett Day gig at the Fruitmarket, January 14, 2006.]

There was quite a story behind the first time, because we went to this gig in Aviemore: The Highland Festival put a gig on at 2000 feet, it must have been up in the Mountain Restaurant, and it was part of the Highland Festival and, that would have been around 1999, I think. And they put this outdoor gig on, and it was this Polish theatre company first, and then it was MacFalls Chamber, followed by Martyn

'It's Not the Time You Have...'

Bennett with Cuillin Music. Well, we thought, "great, that's only thirty miles away, we can't miss that!"

So of course, we went along, and we decided that we were going to camp at the bottom of the road—there's a camp site near Loch Morlich. So, we set up our tents there, and we're at that age, you know, you always want to have a couple of drinks, so we walk all the way up the hill to go to this gig. And it was one of the best gigs I've ever been to! You got the whole thing—the theatre company, the music, the setting. The atmosphere was brilliant! I remember the band were great that night, cos Martyn came out into the audience, and danced around, twirling with his pipes, you know, and the audience and everyone dancing, clapping, and really, really high energy stuff! And afterwards he came up to us—that was the first time that we'd properly said "Hello", because he'd seen us at quite a few gigs, turning up and dancing in the front, and, he must have been thinking "who's this bunch?" And then he noticed us at that gig and came up and said, "Hello". And Sorley was straight in there, talking away, and we all said "Hi".

And it was great just to meet him, and he said "Who are you?"

And we said, you know, "we're your fans, and eh, we play in a band," and he was so interested, all of a sudden, "Oh, you play in a band? What is it you do?"

You know, we told him about what we did—he was so interested, and ever since that point of making that connection of us being there, he always had so much enthusiasm for us. When he saw us, it was always, "What are you up to? And what are you doing?" and he'd give us great advice about people, maybe from his own point of view, what sort of mistakes he'd made in the past and maybe what things he thought he could have done better. So it was great to meet him.

Of course after the gig we had to walk back down to the campsite—oh, it must be a good forty-five minutes, an hour's walk. So, when we were walking back down, he must have finished packing up his gear, and all these cars were going

'It's Not the Time You Have...'

back down the road And he was driving a Volvo estate at that time, Kirsten was in the car and he'd sort of got a bit of gear in the back, and he spots us at the side of the road—there were about seven of us. He says, "Oh, you guys, you're not walking down the hill, are you?" And we goes, "Well, yea, we're just staying down at the campsite, you know. It's been a great night, thanks very much."

"Och, jump in the car, come on!"

So, all seven of us [laughs] jump in the back of this Volvo estate—Martyn and Kirsten in the front, with seven teenagers in the back! Some of us had had a wee bit to drink that night as well, so [laughs] I'm sure for him it was quite an experience! We're all sitting arms and legs everywhere, you know, and it was a great thing because we were completely buzzing with this—Oh, we'd been given a lift by Martyn Bennett! He's our idol! Brilliant! You know! We got to the bottom of the road, and of course he dropped us off— that was one of the quite little memories, being in that Volvo all cramped up! I mean there was lots of other gigs we used to go to, and after that time he'd always say hello. And we'd see him afterwards.

We met him—but we never really worked together creatively, we never were in the studio, you know, never worked musically. He got our first album as soon as it was out—and he was always emailing us. Sorley used to keep in contact with him, to keep him updated as to what we were doing, sending emails. And if we had any new music, whatever it was, it was always—we always knew we wanted to get Martyn's opinion on it. You know, it would be, "Let's send Martyn some of that." All of us were sending him different levels, different bits of music, and getting emails back. It was great, you know, to have someone like that just to be able to call on, with such a wealth of experience, and above all, such a great guy with such great energy. It was really good—yea. So over to Misha—

'It's Not the Time You Have...'

Misha: Well taking off from where John was talking—the earlier experiences of Martyn's music... Martyn was—IS—just an impressive character. Over time, as you become more mature as a person, and your ideas develop, and you scratch back the layers, to find out what sets Martyn apart from other music that we loved at the time, and other people we liked, was, we kept discovering another layer to this, you know, deeper, and deeper, and deeper and deeper. From his first album, right the way through to 'Grit'—and still, when you hear a piece of music of his, you're continually hearing new things in that music. It's like, trying to describe whisky, or something—you just can't describe it. I mean, I've never even heard anyone trying to describe whisky, except whisky tasters, they might try and describe it, but no-one can describe it accurately, because the taste is just so deep, and very difficult to describe. [laughs] And I think that's what's so amazing about Martyn's music, you can listen to it time and time again, and you still keep hearing it. Of course that's a mark of his depth as a person as well. There are so many talented musicians in Scotland, but what set Martyn apart was the vision that he was able to take, and the pictures he was able to paint. Sometimes I look at Martyn's music as a metaphor for the solutions, in politics, in Scottish culture—in every aspect of Scottish culture where you've got the parochial aspects, the fact that there's such a resistance to keep these traditions from changing, and as a result, they can often die out. Sometimes I think that folk music has become the preserve of the middle classes, it's become a recital of something that people have learned, and they're not really connected to it. And I think that Martyn addressed that straight on. For me, it really is an inspiration to have these thoughts, to think of Martyn, and think of the things he had to say as a person, as a character, and through his music—the two become the same thing.

You get a huge sense of the fact that he himself came from the depth of tradition, that he knew it inside out, and he

'It's Not the Time You Have...'

knew which parts of the tradition were the vital things. The spirit is the key —and how that tradition is addressed and how it changes over time is a different matter. But the spirit within that tradition is there. The fact that he had such a complete understanding, and had such a solid grounding in it, is what gave him the confidence to be able to go out there and to play with it. And to challenge people's opinions—that's why Martyn was such a character to respect because you knew he thought everything through. He was saying something that was well thought out, whether again it was musical or in a conversation or whatever—definitely.

The times I spent talking to him, Martyn was always as quick as possible, as keen as possible, to get to the deepest part of the conversation, to cut through the small talk. I would say I have not spoken to Martyn a huge number of times but we have an understanding because he could see we're coming from the same perspective and working on the same ideas. We come from a background of tradition, that values tradition, [but not set in cement or stone?] Yea, that is right. And we come from two cultures as well, so it gives perspective on each one—you can see it more completely if you are further away from it.

The fact that Martyn had a poetic vision at the same time as his musical talent was the important thing.

Margaret: That's an interesting point. I was talking to Raymond Ross—he did a lot with Hamish Henderson and other poets and also worked with Martyn—and he asked about the Martyn Bennett Day at Celtic Connections. And Raymond said, "I hope they are not forgetting the stuff he did on Sorley [MacLean]'s poetry [Hallaig], or Hamish's poetry [Floret Sylva Undique]..." Because Martyn used to listen intently to every word, the meaning, the depth, the layers of the meaning you talk of?

Misha: That is absolutely right. I think with poets—of course not as a rule, but generally—they tend to have a deep source of meaning.

'It's Not the Time You Have...'

But when people listen to poetry, there is less of the appreciation of the technical aspect in poetry than is in music. Music can be so easily tight in the technical side, which, of course, Martyn had brilliantly. But what is so rare is that poetic vision. And to combine the two is something that is so rare. But to combine in such strong quantities of whatever is just brilliant—it's inspirational to me.

We listen to the songs as well, 'Grit' and 'Glen Lyon'— we listen to the whole thing. I really think the ideas that Martyn took to Scottish music are key—in the foregrounds of the music, the simple idea and the detail is in the background. With a lot of earlier folk and traditional music, or a lot of traditional music as it's played now, the detail is in the foreground, not in the background. It can be the too obvious— all very difficult to start to describe, but that's how I think about it.

Margaret: I know he was very fond of Croft No. Five— "they've got it," he said and that really thrilled him immensely. He was not the one to keep glory for himself; if he could give away anything, he would. He was very generous in that sense.

Misha: He certainly was—certainly was…Now, we do a couple of tracks of his music—'Sputnik in Glen Sheil' and 'Four Notes', they've both been re-arranged so the tracks are in constant evolution. It's a real shame that we never managed to work with Martyn, though he was in the studio a few times when we were recording… A lot of the challenges that he has faced and overcome are things that we are in the process of understanding or have yet to come across. So in that sense we still have a tremendous amount to learn from him in listening to his music.

'It's Not the Time You Have...'

MARYANN KENNEDY, Gaelic singer, (Cliar) and broadcaster (BBC Scotland, Celtic Connections), conversation, Glasgow, January 2006:

Maryann: Around the time that 'Grit' was about to come out, I went over to the house in Mull, and I did an hour-long interview, which was fantastic... Not long afterwards I phoned to say, "D'you know who's in today, in our studio, in Ardgour? Croft No. Five, and they're going to record a session for Celtic Connections, they're going to record an EP with Glaswegian rappers called 'Damaged Goods'." And even though he was on the phone, I swear I could hear his ears pricking up! And I said, "If I came for you and I brought you back, and I know that Kirsten will have my head on my hands if I don't look after you to the Nth degree, would you like to come over and just listen to the music and see the boys, because they would so love to have you around?" And so, that's exactly what happened, I brought him over, he was in great form, he so enjoyed seeing the 'crofters' and it wasn't just a rapper, à la hip-hop, it was an entire Glaswegian posse—I've never seen so many people in the control room at Watercolour! And he was a very special part of the music that happened that day, and we did another interview with him again, where he was every bit as generous—the same opinions came out differently. I'm so glad that I have those two interviews side by side because it was him on a glorious day—he summed so many things up for me. I felt glad to have had that day with him.

Margaret: Now, you come from a long line of tradition, did you feel that he also knew tradition from the depths?

Maryann: You know, when I first heard and listened to Martyn's music, I wasn't sure. It was only when I met him and talked to him that I realized, "*O a' bhalaich,* [Oh boy!] You have it! You understand it!" And it was when I'd asked him "What do you say to people who accuse you of mucking about with the music?" he explained to me, "Well, I think the source recordings, the tradition, and all of that that's there, is so precious, and so wonderful, I want to give it to other people, but I know that if I give it to them as raw material they're going to hold their hands up in horror and go 'what's that?' And so part of what my music is, is a way of opening other people's eyes, ears, minds to that." That was the point at which I thought, "I'm yours forever, Martyn, I completely understand where you're coming from." You know, I was up there, in the top whatever, of the fan-base after that!

Margaret: Maryann, you were probably one of the last people to work with Martyn—you had *him* behind the microphone.

Maryann: I did. He had been very much involved with a project investigating the possible links between the Presbyterian Gaelic psalm singing that we are familiar with and similar traditions in Alabama. And he had been so enthusiastic, because what Martyn was really totally carried away with was the depth and musicality and spirituality of what was in the Gaelic psalm singing—he understood it for what it was— the Gaelic psalm is at the heart of 'Liberation' (on 'Grit'). What happened was, that Calum Martin (from Lewis) brought together a dozen or so precentors to record them with as big of a congregation that he could muster, at psalm singing that wasn't a church service. And Martyn encouraged me to go to that because he thought it was going to be a really important night, and that people should be there to hear it. And so he himself was there, with Kirsten, and I was there because, from having spoken to him, I just thought I had to be there—that's what Martyn had for me. Anyway, everyone that was *deònach* [willing] turned up to sing in an enormous church, and the sound was quite amazing.

Margaret: Yes, it was fantastic, and thrilling to be part of that congregation! And out of this came the series of television programmes, with you as interviewer—

Maryann: Yes, and Martyn remained very much involved in the whole television project that had kind of spun out from the original recordings that were made at Back Free Church in the

Isle of Lewis. But he was so very ill in the very last interview. And on one level I felt so bad for going to the house knowing that he was going to find this incredibly difficult, to muster the energy, and it would leave him wasted afterwards. I said, "This will only be a very short time, and if you don't want to do it—" wanting to back off and give him the chance to do the same because I used to get really annoyed at people who would come and sook up his energy, cos Martyn would switch himself on—he wanted to entertain, to open up, to give, to be enthusiastic all the time, even when he was ill. But after that interview, my very last, I came away with the biggest smile on my face... Martyn just made me alive after speaking to him— he was so open and generous with his spirit, with opinions, with his thoughts, with his sense of humour, with his twinkly eyes... he also understood—he had that ability about him.

CALUM MARTIN, musician, song-maker, Gaelic Psalm project leader, Tong, Isle of Lewis. Email, January. 2006:

During one of our long telephone conversations, when we were discussing the track 'Liberation'[55], Martyn was telling me about one of his many setbacks with regard to copyright problems.[56] And just when he was really at the point of giving up on 'Liberation', I mentioned to him that both Murdina and Effie were still alive and living on Lewis; one in the village of Ballantrushal on the west side of the island, and Effie in Achmore. He was amazed to hear this news, as he had imagined that they had long passed away.

He was really excited when I asked him if he would like to meet one or both of them and he said, "that would be great, Calum. Do you think you could make it happen?"

I promised him I would try, and this I was able to do, via a mutual friend of ours, Donald Murdo Smith who had been a close neighbour of Murdina and Effie.

When Martyn and Kirsten came up to Lewis it was decided that he would visit Murdina in Ballantrushal and maybe

'It's Not the Time You Have...'

leave Effie till another time. He then asked me if it would be OK to see her on his own. This I totally understood and I told him that was fine by me. Before he went over to meet her, he phoned me from Stornoway to ask if it would be OK to buy a CD player so that he could play the track for Murdina. I told him, "No way, Martyn!! She will have a heart attack if you let her hear that! Some of us Presbyterians have a real problem with rhythm and drums," and, teasing him, I told him, "if it was a Country and Western tune you might stand a chance! But seeing Murdina probably has no television or radio she will think that this is—I don't know what she will think!!" A hearty laugh from Martyn followed, and he said "OK! I take your point." But I still think he would have loved to have done it!!

I spoke to him after the visit and he told me that they hit it off so well. I think there was a kindred spirit, because, in many ways they were similar, in that they had both done something which, in its day, was seen as rather controversial—Martyn with his Urban beats mixed with sampled Gaelic Psalms and Murdina and Effie doing something which had not been done before: Women precenting and recording and taking the Psalms outside a Church, till that time totally male dominated.

He left Murdina's house with a satisfied smile—and under his arm a heavy-duty book on Theology, which he promised he would read. She had given him her blessing—and the rest, as they say with regard to 'Liberation', is history.

But even before then, we had many conversations about the 'Liberation' track, Gaelic Psalm Singing, and about the album in general. In fact, as I said, at one point he had decided that, because of all the hassle with getting permission for various samples that he would have to forget about the 'Liberation' track completely.

He was feeling tired and fed up, so I told him to think about using other voices for the Gaelic Psalms—I suggested we try out two or three of the, (shall we say maturer) female voices, that were able to sing Gaelic Psalms, but he came back to me later saying he would rather try out one of the new young Gaelic singers, I was sceptical, but as it turned out, this was something that never happened anyway. He subsequently asked me if I would like to try myself. I felt a bit reticent but agreed, so he sent me up the backing tracks and I had a bash. I soon realised that this was something that could not be captured in a sterile studio situation, however good the voices were. Nevertheless, I sent the recordings back to him—reluctantly. I later phoned him and told him that in my view it was Murdina and Effie or nothing. He agreed, but then cheekily said, "Do you want to hear what I have done with your recording? I think it sounds quite good."

I said "OK", thinking he was only joking! A couple of days later, a CD arrived in the post. This is now a rare, (thankfully), one of a kind, recording which will remain solely in my possession unless I am being blackmailed! The backing on the original recording of 'Liberation' was very different (much darker and heavier), and was never going to happen because of all the legal loopholes with copyright and impossible financial demands from some of the sampled artists and those who recorded them. But from the ashes came (in my view) an even better version with the great voice of Michael Marra capturing the feel of the track in a special way—only Martyn could have done it. What a guy!!! What a triumph!!!

One final memory I have of him is when, during a visit to my home in Tong, Martyn, Kirsten and I decided to take a walk down to the beach. It was a nice evening but a bit cold and as we walked along the beach from Tong towards Back, Martyn began to get really excited about all the various rock formations and water pools on the shoreline. He was jumping from the rocky outcrops down onto the beach with wild abandon forgetting about his medical condition "Watch your back!" said Kirsten with a look of concern. Ignoring her pleas to be careful, he said, "Look at this amazing rock formation—my Dad would love this!" Kirsten and I looked at each other and shrugged our shoulders. I'm sure he would have spent ages staring in wonderment at something that the vast majority of us would not give a second glance to—but that was Martyn.

'It's Not the Time You Have...'

All of a sudden he said quietly, "I think we better go home now," and that was when Kirsten noticed that the circulation had stopped in his hands. Back home and warmed by the fire he was soon back on form playing my Martin Acoustic Guitar, and in a zone of his own. "This is the best sounding guitar I have ever played!" he said. I never found out if he was really telling the truth on that one. "I can't really play guitar," he added modestly—but this was not a mere guitarist but an amazing musical genius with perfect pitch, tuning the guitar to the modal DADGAD tuning and 'pottering around' as he called it. Soon he began to tire and he said "I think I need my bed.

I will always remember that special evening.

Thanks, Martyn, for all the memories.

NOTES FROM THE CD 'SALM AND SOUL',[57] produced by Calum Martin, 2005:

The photograph of Martyn on 'Salm and Soul' (also on the front cover of this book) was gifted by Canada's 'Portrait Photographer of the Year 2005', **Manon Rousso**. Her exhibition, *'Galerie'*, which can be viewed on-line, includes two portraits of Martyn, *'Concert Intime'* [Intimate Concert] and *'Le Violon Bleu'* [the Blue Violin].[58]

To quote Manon herself, *"La photographie à mes yeux, c'est un moment précieux, empreint d'amour et d'émotions, si intense et fixé dans le temps pour l'éternité."* [Photography in my eyes is a way to capture a precious instant in time. It can be very intense or ephemeral, but it becomes fixed in time for eternity.]

CALUM MARTIN'S DEDICATION OF THE CD 'SALM AND SOUL', September 2005:

This CD is dedicated to the memory of Martyn Bennett, musician and composer extraordinaire, a true friend to all who knew him. Martyn's brilliant innovative musical talent was totally inspirational to so many musicians—he did it first and he did it best; he was imitated, but never bettered. He also loved the Gaelic Psalms and was hugely supportive of the efforts being made to raise vital funds for the Bethesda Hospice in Stornoway, Isle of Lewis. As a cancer sufferer himself, he knew first-hand how special a place this really was.

But maybe his most important gift to us all was that Martyn was first and foremost, a beautiful humble, human being, devoid of ego, with an extraordinary sensitive and loving spirit, which he conveyed to all in his company by an aura, which constantly surrounded him. It was a real privilege to have known him for these briefest of moments in life's journey.

'It's Not the Time You Have...'

POEMS AND SONGS FOR THE MUSIC-MAKER

Gaisgeach Og a' Chuil: Mar Chuimhneachan air Martainn
(Domhnall Meek)

Chuir an gaisgeach òg
An ceòl na chridhe,
Agus a chridhe sa cheòl;
Chuir e gleus ùr air an spiorad,
Neart biothbhuan
Ann an co-sheirm Alba.

Gabhaidh e a thuras deireannach
Di-Satharna
Do Mhuile àlainn,
Do Chalgaraidh grianach na mara,
Agus ni e ceòl ris na dùilean
A chruthaich Righ nan Dùil -
Gàir nan cuantan,
Osnadh na gaoithe,
Gairm nan eun,
A mhiann sàsaichte
Ann an co-sheirm na Gàidhlig.

Cluinnidh sinn e
Agus cuimhnichidh sinn air,
Air a threuntas
Agus air a charathannas,
Agus nar cridhe-ne
Bidh an gaisgeach òg
Ceòlmhor
Beò gu siorraidh.

Composed by Donald E. Meek, Edinburgh (and Tiree) —'a few lines in Martyn's memory, as a tribute to him...' February 2005.

'It's Not the Time You Have...'

Translation:
    Young Lion of Music: In memory of Martyn

        The young lion
        Took music to his heart,
        Put his heart in music,
        New-tuning the spirit,
        Re-energising for ever
        The harmony of Scotland.

        He will make his last journey
        On Saturday
        To his beloved Mull,
        To sun-kissed Calgary by the sea,
        Making music with elements
        By their Ruler created –
        The sound of the sea,
        The sigh of the wind,
        The cries of the birds;
        His dreams fulfilled
        In the harmony of Gaelic.

        We will hear him,
        We will remember him
        For his courage
        And generosity,
        For his love
        And in our hearts
        The young champion of Music
        Will live forever.

Translated by Bill Innes, Glasgow (and South Uist), 2005

'It's Not the Time You Have...'

Oran do Mhàrtainn

(Calum Martainn)

Tha mi nis a' caoidh an òglaich,
fear cho grinn le nàdar òirdhearc
'S e dh'fhàg mi gu dubhach brònach,
an là sheòl e mach à sealladh.

Sèist: O nach robh mi thall 's na beannan,
le mo charaid ceòl is rannan,
O nach robh mi thall 's na beannan.

2. Bha mi 'n dùil bhom thaobh nach gluaiseadh,
am fear grinn a rinn ar stiùireadh
Nuair bha dùil air ais san dùthaich,
's ann a bha a chuairt aig deireadh.

3. Bha a thàlant mar an siùcar,
milis mar a' ghrian a' dùsgadh,
Bhith na chuideachd 's e cho cùiseach,
sona ann bho oidhch' gu madainn.

4. Nochd an tinneas grànnda tùrsach,
dhan a bheath nuar nach robh dùil ris,
Dh'ainideoin sin, le pian is ùpraid,
cha robh gearran aig a' bhalach.

5. Thànig meas 'n dèidh a' chaochlaidh,
mar is tric sin dòigh an t-saoghail,
Ged a bha an t-urram cùbhaidh,
b' fheàrr a bhith gun duais 's e againn.

6. Ille ghrinn bha coibhneil sìobhalt,
ged nach fhaic sinn ann an tìm thu,
Bidh ar cuimhne ort cho prìseil,
fhad 's a bhios sinn tarraing anail.

'It's Not the Time You Have...'

Translation
Song for Martyn

      I now lament the young man,
      One so fine, of splendid nature;
      It left me sad and grieving
      That day he sailed from sight.

Chorus: Oh, that I could be in the hills
               With my friend in music and song,
               Oh, that I could be in the hills.

2.   I wished with all my heart that
      Our inspiration had not left us,
      Just when we hoped for his return
      Was when his journey ended.

3.   His talent was as sweet
      As the rising of the sun,
      To be in his expert company
      Passed the night happy until dawn.

4.   The ugly, grievous illness struck
      His life when least expected;
      Despite that, and pain and distress,
      No complaint was heard or uttered.

5.   Esteem came after his death -
      So often the way of the world;
      Though the honour was welcome
      We would gladly trade it for his presence.

6.   Fine young man, so kind and gentle
      Though we won't see you in our time,
      Our memories will be so precious
      As long as we draw breath.

'It's Not the Time You Have...'

Calum Martin, Tong Isle of Lewis, composed the song (words and music) in 2005, and recorded it with his daughter Ishbel Ann (accompanied by Malcolm Jones of Runrig) on 'Salm and Soul' (volume 3 of the Gaelic Psalm CD series). Having became close friends through the Gaelic Psalm project, Calum and Martyn shared thoughts, ideas, laughter, tunes, songs, and, above all, their love of the Gaelic Psalms and a wonderful kinship.

Haiku for Martyn

Music soaks the earth
Flooding through peat and heather
Every rock sounding

MURDO MACDONALD, 4 February 2005

GEORGE BENNETT, Martyn's grandfather, played the first set of bagpipes Martyn ever heard. They shared a love of the hills [59] (especially the Cuillins), of bikes, of piobearachd and of words—poems, songs, or just words. They discussed electronics and 'soundscapes', as grandfather introduced grandson to the ground-breaking work of R. Murray Schafer with its provocative opening statement: 'Overheard in the lobby after the première of Beethoven's *Fifth:* "Yes, but is it music?"'[60] They agreed that 'Captain Carswell' must be among the best ever marches, but didn't agree about wearing red shoes with the kilt, or about bending notes, or that 'fast doesn't necessarily equal good'. Show me, who makes the rules? Why can't you wear what you like? And, 'just for Papi'[61]—if you're going to play fast, then go on, play fast! But be GOOD at playing fast!

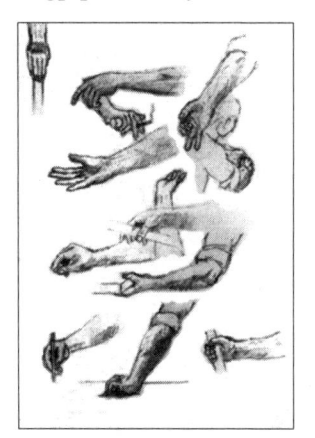

'It's Not the Time You Have...'

A little poem from memory, recited on the telephone, then emailed from Halifax, Nova Scotia.

Perhaps
                           Author unknown

Perhaps if you could see
The splendour of the land
To which our loved ones have gone
From you and me—you'd understand.

Perhaps if you could hear
The welcome they receive
From old familiar voices
All so dear—you would not grieve.

Perhaps if you could know
The reason why they went
You'd wipe away those tears that flow
And wait—content.

Sìth do d' anam, is clach air do chàrn[62]

'It's Not the Time You Have…'

Acknowledgements

My sincere thanks to **Colin Hynd**, Director of Celtic Connections for all his support over the years, and for creating 'Martyn Bennett Day', January 2006. Warmest appreciation to all the musicians who worked so hard to make it happen. My thanks to all who gave me 'Martyn stories' to record, and to folk who emailed or sent theirs. Thanks also to **Dougie Anderson** at Coda Music for his encouragement—'a wee bookie would be a good idea…' and to **Gonzalo Mazzei** of Grace Note Publications without whom this 'wee book' might never have been published.

Drawings, Sketches & Music Notation

All the drawings and musical quotations are from Martyn's own notebooks and/or sketches, apart from the one line of music from Capt. John MacLellan (page 20). The Gaelic song quotations are all from Martyn's transcriptions of Newfoundland fieldwork recordings (see notes 17 & 42).

'It's Not the Time You Have...'

'It's Not the Time You Have...'

NOTES, SCRIBBLES & OTHER RAMBLINGS

Now and again, when writing an article or book, I would ask Martyn to help me with some footnote or other. It was usually about music, for, even in his early teens, I valued his observation, insight, perception and awareness. Such was the request I made one time, when he said, "OK, just leave it for me —I'll do the footnotes for you..." He did, but when I went through the manuscript, it soon became apparent that he had added quite a number of his own—little footnotes, each one drawn carefully sitting on a small musical stave, perfect little feet, black, white, some dotted... and a note to tell me "footnotes added as requested".

[1] Martyn died on the last night of Celtic Connections 2005—January 30.

[2] I came upon these words quite by chance—or so it seemed—in a little book of quotations left beside the space once filled by Martyn's mixing desk—*100 Ways to Keep Your Soul Alive*. Curiously, the page was flagged by a little yellow 'post-it'. (The original is from Edward C. Sellner's *Mentoring—The Ministry of Spiritual Kinship*, 1990, p.145.)

[3] Singer, song-maker, multi-instrumentalist, writer, and former front man of Battlefield Band, Brian is also Head of Scottish Music at the Royal Scottish Academy of Music and Drama. In July 2005, when the RSAMD posthumously conferred an Honorary Doctorate on Martyn, Brian gave the honorary address. Resplendent in academic gowns (instead of Harley-Davidson T-shirt) Brian began his tribute with 'Lord Chairman, Principal, Governors of the Academy, Members of the Academic Board, Ladies and Gentlemen, I stand before you today to celebrate an extraordinary artistic life...'

[4] Martyn was born in St. John's, Newfoundland, Feb. 17, 1971, on his dad's 24th birthday. Though his officially registered birth name was Martyn Bennett-Knight, there was never any discussion (so far as I know) about why, or when, Martyn decided to shorten it. No asking parents' opinion or permission, no informing either of them. No

'It's Not the Time You Have...'

questions of normal procedures or protocol (if there was such a thing). No fuss. Oblivious to the element of surprise or curiosity within the family, the possibility of indignation, or that there might be anything unusual about an eleven year-old altering his name—it was a *fait accompli*.

Martyn's attitude to modifying or changing his own name seemed to epitomize his approach to life. The 'right way' was a matter of opinion—someone else's opinion. He could learn the rules, but that did not mean he'd agree to keep them in any circumstances, barring two—Captain John MacLellan's piping lessons and the disciplined classical orchestra. Everything else was open to question, negotiation, adjustment or modification—rhythm, beat, variations on melody and all else besides. Recipes—never mind the visitors, taste it! Clothes—this is a great wee sewing machine. Furniture arrangements—that was in a stupid place to begin with! Light fittings—come on, they were a fire hazard! Too late—they're in the bin. Someone else's bicycle saddle and handlebars: What do you mean, permission? Mum, it's a surprise! You'll love it—you'll wish you'd done it years ago...'

Explaining made no difference. Martyn's peripheral vision never seemed to catch the impact such changes might have on others, far less the frustration or even havoc he might cause.

As for discussing the name? If his mother happened to be sitting on the grass at the Nethybridge Highland Games beside his piping teacher, then she was in good company when she heard the announcement. 'David, did I hear him say the next competitor is Martyn Bennett?' But David Taylor, well ahead of me, seemed taken aback by my surprise: 'That's what Martyn puts on all his school notebooks.'

So that was that. I knew I would have to wait for the right moment to raise this topic, so when we moved from Kingussie to Edinburgh three years later, with pen in hand I asked: 'What should I put on this form for the music school?'

'Put Bennett,' ran the conversation. 'But if I'd thought more about it I'd have put Stewart in the first place. And maybe I should have the Gaelic spelling, M-a-r-t-a-i-n-n.'

'Really? Why? You're winding me up here?'

'Because I belong to that family. Skye is where we always go—Glenconon, where Granny comes from. Our traditions come from there. But just write Bennett.'

'It's Not the Time You Have...'

'Wait a minute—have you talked to your Dad about this? Or have you realized that if you just use my maiden name, everyone might think you were illegitimate?

'Oh for goodness sake, I don't believe you're saying this! Listen, Dad said the spelling of Martyn is Welsh, so that's OK. And Papi was a good piper. So leave it simple. Martyn Bennett.'

5   Mariposa, 1975—we shared a week in Toronto with wonderful 'native peoples', our children playing together at the festival and in the hotel at night. I thought we slept through the all-night drumming, but maybe Martyn was counting the beats!

6   Dismayed at the far-back seats we had in Glasgow's Old Athenaeum, (to tell the truth, disgusted at the person who chose them—'I can't see a thing from here!') he took off by himself to find an empty one above the orchestra pit. ('You'll be fine by yourself, Mum...')

7   The theme of the piece is based on 'Lament for Mary MacLeod' a favourite pibroch of Dr Kenneth Mackay of Laggan who devoted his working life to a medical mission Peru. Martyn's composition was inspired by Dr Mackay's diary of his journey through the Andes, his reflection on Scottish music as he listened to the Peruvian pipes and adapted to a new culture. The piece opens with Psalm 121 and features the pipes of both countries, along with voices, clarsach and the classical orchestra.

8   Martyn played around with echoes in the late 1980s in the damp, unlit, echoey basement vaults of Linlithgow Palace. We were whiling away a Sunday afternoon, 'being tourists' then having fun singing and playing with echoes in the eerie space. (Never mind the tourists, doesn't everyone sing in dark palace vaults?) Not unusually, I had a reel-to-reel Uher in the car, so the unstoppable Martyn fetched it, microphone stand and all. "OK, now, sing!" And so I did, if only to get out of the pitch-dark corner I was in.

9   Brian's speech ended with, 'I therefore ask the Principal to confer the degree of Doctor of Music (honoris causa) upon Martyn

Bennett and invite Kirsten Bennett to come forward and accept the degree on behalf of Martyn.'

[10] The first set of bellows pipes Martyn saw was in Kingussie—my cousin John MacRae, a fine piper himself, had a beautiful old set that has been in the family for many years. (He was a neighbour of Hamish Moore who was the local vet in Kingussie at the time). Martyn loved these pipes and when we moved to Edinburgh he drew them from memory to explain to me of how they were made—and if we ever found a set, maybe...? Shortly afterwards Colin Ross brought a set of bellows pipes to the School of Scottish Studies to be delivered to Willie Haines at Blackfriars Music. Martyn happened to be there, having called in on his way home from school, and was only too keen to volunteer to take the pipes to Blackfriars Street for Colin. (He said he'd look after them while he was waiting for his mother to come out of the 5 o'clock lecture.) Before the pipes ever left George Square, however, Martyn was playing them and could hardly wait to let Willie hear the beautiful tone. And it was Willie Haines, not his mother, who said, 'the pipes are yours, Martyn.' I have to confess it's a real test of composure (and friendship) when someone steamrolls over your (perceived) 'parent role' and says 'Never mind your mother! Don't listen to her!' (Thanks a lot, Willie, and this time I mean it!) As Willie well remembers, he just laughed at my 'no way, I've just bought a violin and a piano, and if you think—' Undaunted, Martyn said he'd busk every Saturday to pay for them and Willie (I thought in mock seriousness) set up an account for him. Week after week, smartly dressed, he'd set off to Princes Street with his Highland pipes. After busking for an hour the first Saturday, he discovered the pipe box was too heavy to carry to Willie's shop. Those were the days of phone boxes so I got to watch the pantomime of Martyn and Willie counting the coins—over £25 an hour in those days seemed phenomenal for an adult far less a thirteen year-old and the debt was cleared in jig time. A couple of years later (and a few inches taller) when Martyn's earnings were drastically reduced, he discovered the first the rule of busking: The smaller you are, the more you earn.

[11] These drawings are a selected from a notebook Martyn kept on the trip with David.

'It's Not the Time You Have...'

[12]   PS from Kingussie: Just for the record, Martyn's first paid gig was, nevertheless, in Kingussie—Kath and David Russell who ran the 'Wooden Spoon Restaurant' were only too pleased to have him pipe in the New Year in 1982. Kath recalled, "He was so tiny we had to stand him on a table! Imagine asking the piper stand on a table at Hogmanay! The place was jumping! Just unforgettable!"

[13]   Joe was Martyn's step-father.

[14]   From a notebook, age 7.

[15]   Martyn actually sang an excerpt of this on the documentary made by Artworks Scotland in 2004.

[16]   Sadly, Gordon died in December, 2005—a huge loss to the world of piping.

[17]   When Martyn recorded his arrangement of 'Swallowtail' on his first CD, not surprisingly, none of the reviews picked up the possibility of earlier influences than the 'Edinburgh scene'. In fact Martyn's dad played the 'Swallowtail Reel' in the early '70s with two other musicians. (A classically taught violinist, Ian took up the fiddle after moving to Newfoundland in 1970.) At the time, we lived between two communities, both with very vibrant traditional music scenes. Ian and I were both at graduate school, (he in Geology, and I in Folklore) at Memorial Univeristy of Newfoundland in St. John's. There was no shortage of enthusiastic musicians, many of them fellow students— fiddlers and button-box accordionists who played 'Newfoundland-style' (strongly influenced by three centuries of Irish settlers), along with a number of emigrants, many Irish, who added various styles of music, including whistle and bodhran, to the local sounds. Established groups were part of the scene, such as the Sons of Erin, Figgy Duff, and Ryan's Fancy, who had one of Ireland's champion whistle-players from the sixties, Dennis Ryan whose recording of the 'Swallowtail Reel' was very popular in Canada in the early seventies. I will leave it to the child psychologists to speculate on the influence of what children hear from infancy. I have, however, discussed the subject of how tunes are passed on, both inside and outside the family—Ref. 'From Kennedy Fraser to

the Jimmy Shandrix Experience in Five Generations' in Fintan Vallely's *Crosbhealach an Cheoil: The Crossroads Conference: Tradition and Change*, (Dublin, 1999). Martyn scrutinised my paper before it went to print, and set me right on several points. One aspect that both of us missed, however, concerns the impact of the Newfoundland Gaelic community on his style of playing and repertoire: granted, he spent his first four years there, but, perhaps of considerable significance must the fact that, at the age of 17, he transcribed the music of all the Gaelic songs I recorded, as he helped me publish them in my book, *The Last Stronghold,* (Canongate, Edinburgh and Breakwater, St. John's, 1989). As anyone who has transcribed will know, it takes a lot of concentrated listening, hour after hour, to do it accurately. One of the songs he transcribed for me was *'Oran nam Mogaisean'* (the Mocassin Song) which he asked me to sing for the album 'Glen Lyon'. To tell the truth, he insisted I sang it—'Never mind the questions, just sing it.' So of course I did… I only wish we had a video of my reaction, and his, when he first let me hear a recording of what he did with it! I was completely wowed—and Martyn just smiled.

[18] It was truly a lifelong friendship for Martyn as he and Cathal first met around 1973, at the Mariposa Festival in Toronto.

[19] This is the Dr Kenneth MacKay (1899—1987) whose name is celebrated on Martyn's orchestral composition, 'MacKay's Memoirs' (see note 7).

[20] The entire week was spent in rehearsal at Merchiston Castle in Edinburgh, preparing for a grand concert at the end of it.

[21] While still in his teens Martyn would make light of playing for 'a wee gig with a fairly good scratch band'—for example, in the orchestra pit playing for an opera or ballet. Usually Miles Baster, his teacher at the RSAMD, set it up for him, bringing him in at the last minute to replace a violinist or viola player who was ill or couldn't make it. Now and again he'd ask if I wanted a ticket—'you can pick it up at the box office, but I won't see you, and don't wait for me after the concert.' Seemed like a good deal to me, and whether it was the 'scratch band' or the Youth Orchestra it was fairly normal for the players to get

together after the show. Coming from a world of traditional music which has few, if any, dictates about formal dress code (except in piping), Martyn was nevertheless meticulous, to the last detail, about dress code for an orchestral concert. As there was never any question who'd choose the formal attire, my role in acquiring it was minimal—'keep your eye open for DJs with silk lapels—I don't want one like everyone else's... you don't expect me to wear *that* bow-tie, do you? You're joking! Nobody but *nobody* wears clip-on bow-ties...' And since teaching anyone to tie a 'proper' bow-tie was not one of his mother's skills, he acquired a diagram of 'How to tie a bow-tie'. After several hilarious attempts, he announced success, demonstrating by deftly tying it around his knee—'now to learn to do this round my neck,' said he. When I asked who in the world (or the audience) was going to notice whether it was clipped on or tied, he was amazed at my limited knowledge of after-concert etiquette. 'We all go to the pub afterwards, and as soon as we get there, Miles and all these old guys loosen their bow-ties, have a glass of wine and relax. But what about me? I've got to keep *two* bow ties, one to clip on at the concert and the *proper* one rolled up in my pocket, so I can dive into the gents, take off the clip-on bow and emerge with the other one draped round my neck like the others... No, I've got learn how to tie this!'

[22]   There's a photo of Martyn, around the age of 13, playing his small pipes in Sorley's house in Skye while standing in front of a portrait drawing of Sorley himself. Also, it was probably around the time Anna Wendy talks of that Martyn was asked to compose a tune in honour of Sorley's 75th birthday and play it at a special event during the National Mod in Edinburgh. Then, in the intervening years between school orchestra days and when Martyn composed the music for Hallaig, there were many events when he heard Sorley read the poem.

[23]   The remainder of the conversation with Anna Wendy was not so much about music-making with Martyn, but about the complexity of the common experiences they shared in their family backgrounds. Though very different in countless ways, both acknowledged the crucial part played by the lifelong family experiences that nurtured them. This was not the sort of discussion I had had with Martyn as it was much more fitting for him to share it with Anna Wendy. Her own candidness

is a gift, and her reflective observations on this subject are vitally important to her music and indeed to the wider world of music-making and the study of its influences. We need only listen to 'Gowd & Silver', her CD with her grandfather, Ronald Stevenson (Ecclectic ECL CD 0518), or, better still, a concert performance of both of them, to sense the profound depth of what Anna Wendy describes. (On her new CD Anna Wendy plays 'Mull Wedding' composed by Martyn's dad, Ian Knight.) www.anna-wendy.com

[24] Raymond's play 'The Haunting of Billy Marshall' was probably the first theatre piece or drama for which Martyn composed. Other works included Tom McGrath's adaptation of Robert Louis Stevenson's 'Kidnapped' (The Lyceum, produced by Kenny Ireland, 1995); David Harrower's 'Knives in Hens' (The Traverse Theatre, 1996); a six-part TV series, 'Burns Alive and Kicking' scripted by Chris Dolan for Caledonia, Stern and Wilde's Channel 4 production; 'The Grey Selkie o' Sule Skerry' scripted for radio drama by Barbara McDermitt (1993); 'Urisks', a five-part animated TV series about Gaelic mythological characters (Leslie MacKenzie of West Highland Animation, for Gaelic TV, 1995); a musical score for the Gaelic TV drama, 'Ag Iasgach' (The Fishing, 1996); 'The Real Wild West', a sit-com by David Cosgrove for Mull Theatre, 2000; and 'Bairns' Bothers', a French mono-drama by Raymond Cousse, translated by Bill Findlay for Mull Theatre, 2000. Then there were the TV ads, such as the Drambuie commercial (composed while he was still in his teens), Scots Porage Oats among others.

In the early years, several of the dramas seemed to take up residence in our drawing room, as Martyn would 'live' the story for weeks. (There was the memorable battle scene from Kidnapped, all clashing swords choreographed to clashing music—Come till you hear this! What's that sword doing here? What do you think? What do you mean, there's nowhere to sit down for all these instruments? Sit? Is there something wrong with the living room? I didn't invite you to *sit*, I invited you to listen!) Even when he got his first flat at Tollcross, in which he built a tiny studio, he'd return to raid bookshelves, pilfer recordings, vinyl, reels, or cassettes, though occasionally, (and usually because he couldn't locate it himself), he might resort to asking permission for some gem he suspected he'd seen somewhere in his

'It's Not the Time You Have...'

mother's archive collection. As Kirsten would later testify, when Martyn was composing he'd seem far away, deep in thought, oblivious to the world around him, to room temperature, hunger or even thirst—'I never heard you say dinner was ready! You didn't call me if it was...' Nevertheless, he'd tidy it all up afterwards, as he loved order, and also loved to cook.

[25] Since the Scotsman Diary was compiled by, or attributed to, Anthony Troon, Martyn was totally mystified at this. He didn't suspect Raymond when he came home from school, paper in hand, because the head teacher had called him in to explain this 'thing' in the Diary. Raymond confessed some time later.

[26] While the programme for that day records the key figures who led the protest , it is also a record of one of Martyn's earliest connections with leading figures whose work (and friendship) played a significant part in his life— Piper Martyn Bennett, artists Timothy Neat (representing the Scottish Sculpture Trust) and Will MacLean, and writers Tom McGrath, Brian McCabe and Ron Butler were among them, as were Owen Dudley Edwards, Neil MacCormack and folk already well known to him such as Hamish Henderson and the Stewarts of Blair.

[27] My intention, (as I recall), was to convey the importance of parents listening to children, whether they want to play an instrument, develop a sport, draw, paint, whatever, even if their ideas of what they would like to become may seem out of the ordinary.

[28] Ian Crichton Smith was also a special favourite of Martyn's and so was Edwin Morgan. Also among the older generation was William Montgomerie—after his death, Martyn used to visit his widow, Norah, artist and folklorist, whose children's books he loved. He'd sit by Norah's bed in the nursing home and play his whistle or fiddle for her— just the two of them, as she used to tell me. Caithness poet George Gunn and Martyn planned collaboration, but their proposal was relegated to some file or other—'rejected, failed'. Looking back to some of these earlier poetry readings in Edinburgh, Martyn disguised, or even trivialised, his love of poetry behind an irresistible urge to mimic, not

only the voices but also the mannerisms, in hilarious, yet minimalist, caricatures of the poets.

[29]   www.nva.org.uk

[30]   Martyn was a member of the group, 'Drumalban' (formed by dance expert James MacDonald Reid in the 1970s), which specialises in traditional Scottish dances that pre-date the prescribed styles of the Royal Scottish Country Dance Society (formed 1923) and the Official Board of Highland Dancing (formed 1949). Though he had lessons in Highland dancing from Maggie Moore in Kingussie, he neither owned nor wished to wear any stylised 'Highland games' outfit. He was, however, very interested in the authentic clothing worn by folk who actually danced these older styles. Martyn's first tour as a musician was to Uist, playing for Drumalban.

[31]   The recording of the Glen Lyon Lament was sponsored by *Proiseact nan Ealan* (The Gaelic Arts Project) for Angus's remarkable production 'The Path' which ran for three weeks in Glen Lyon. The song eventually became the title track of Martyn's CD—and the only track to receive any sponsorship. Aside from that track, the complete absence of financial backing (outside of the family) frustrated Martyn and was probably a factor in the delay of the album.

[32]   www.theceilidhplace.com

[33]   A review article in the *Ross-shire Journal* carried the headline, 'Stunning evening of mega-piobearachd' and noted, 'Impossible to categorise and who would to want to anyway, the nearest thing I can get to an overall description of this splendid piece by a prodigiously talented young composer is, mega-piopbearachd.' (Oct. 1996).

[34]   With her letter, Jean sent me the poem, composed by her late husband Robert Urquhart (1923—95, actor) on the death of his son (Matthew George Urquhart, 1957—1974). The most fitting place in this little collection of memories and notes is perhaps on the final page, after the Notes.

[35]   Point is the local name for the Eye Peninsula.

'It's Not the Time You Have...'

[36]   The front cover photo by Manon Rousso was taken in this church.

[37]   Lorraine has performed in the UK many times and, most recently, was guest at the Carrying Stream Festival (celebrating the life of Hamish Henderson) in November 2005. www.greatacoustics.org

[38]   It was for Bennett Hammond that Martyn composed his tune 'Bennett's Blunder' (a joke between them) during one of his visits to Lorraine and Bennett's home in Brookline. Lorraine adds, 'We have a lovely tune, 'Blessings Counted', that Martyn wrote August 1989. That was the summer we were all counting our many blessings.' Bennett also emailed the accompanying sketch Martyn did for him that summer—desert boots, wire rimmed glasses and a box of matches, 'that's just Bennett'.

[39]   The 'Lament for Elizabeth Forbes' is on Sarah's album, 'Chasing the New Moon'—with Martyn on grand piano. He wrote out a complete transcription of his arrangement, suggesting Sarah could save expense by asking someone in Boston to play it. Fortunately she stuck to her plan and recorded it with Martyn.

[40]   Alan Lomax came to one of the shows—the only time Martyn met him. Since early childhood, however, he was well acquainted with two of Lomax's Scottish albums recorded in the 1950s as they were part of our household collection—'Heather and Glen' and 'Folksongs of Scotland' which was Vol. III of the Columbia Records series 'World Library of Folk and Primitive Music'. The original sleeve notes were by Hamish Henderson who travelled with Alan in 1951, but when Rounder re-issued the recording in 1998 (CD1743) I re-wrote the notes with Hamish. In 2001 Lomax's daughter Anna sent the entire Gaelic collection on CDs (more than 300 tracks) when she asked me to select songs and write the notes for new albums. Martyn enjoyed complete access to Lomax's collection though the first album of the new series 'Gaelic Songs of Scotland' was not released till 2006—Rounder CD11661-1785-2, 'Women at Work in the Western Isles'.

[41] A lawyer by profession, Gloria is not only a folk music enthusiast who is involved in, and committed to, promoting Celtic music and musicians in the USA, but she is also an extraordinary photographer.

[42] *Canntaireachd*, which Martyn called 'hee-durrum-haw-durrums' refers to the complex syllabic notation used in teaching the Highland bagpipe. Throughout the history of the instrument, both tunes and techniques of the playing were handed down via this traditional method. The learner not only picks up the tune but also acquires the fingering of it on the pipe chanter. Even today, skilled pipers sing canntaireachd versions to their pupils while teaching them to read the printed musical notation that has become second nature to most pipers. Several examples of *canntaireachd* can also be heard on the cassette produced (1990) from the Newfoundland Gaelic collection that Martyn and I worked on, 'A Codroy Valley Ceilidh with the MacArthur Family: Songs and Music from THE LAST STRONGHOLD' (about to be re-issued on CD, 2006).

[43] 'Belle's Fancy' is part of Martyn's track on 'Grand Concert of Piping' (Greentrax CDTRAX265).

[44] Auchtermuchty Folk Festival is one of the longest running TMSA festivals. Now in its third decade it has long been a favourite gathering place for devotees who look forward to their August get-together with friends who, to many have become their 'folk family'.

[45] Jim, who won the 2005 Scottish Singer of the Year Award (Scot Trad Awards), dedicated his most recent album to Martyn—'Yont the Tay' (Greentrax CDTRAX 272). If only I had had my mini-disc recorder with me when I saw him on the night, we'd also have Jim's colourful, amusing account of this very session.

[46] *Tocher*, No 44, 1992.

[47] Martyn first heard this song in 1975 when we lived in Quebec. Archie Fisher had not long been broadcasting his BBC folk music programmes, and, as a follow-up to a long discussion we'd had at the Mariposa Festival in Toronto, he sent me a cassette of one of his

programmes. It included a feature on Flora, and 'Fhir a Leadan Thlath' was one of the songs she sang. Martyn loved it as much as I did and we'd play it over and over. (I also had Lomax's 1951 recording of 'Mo Run Geal Og.) When he finally met Flora in Scotland, he was so familiar with her voice he felt he knew her—after all, he'd only been in love with her since the age of four.

[48] Martyn's maternal grandmother's family have been rooted in the Trotternish Peninsula of Skye for generations—his great-great grandfather, Peter Stewart whose voice (recorded on wax cylinder, c. 1910) can be heard on two tracks of 'Glen Lyon' was among them. His grandmother, Peigi Stewart (b. 1919, 'Glen Lyon' again) was also born and brought up on the same croft in Glenconon, Uig. Beallach is reached by walking over the hill from that glen—Martyn loved those hills and felt that Glenconon was where his true roots lay.

[49] www.backofthemoon.co.uk

[50] The shortened version is on the notes of the CD *In the Sunny Long Ago...*, Footstompin, CDFSR1708.

[51] Footstompin launched the CD at Celtic Connections Festival 2001, and, thanks to Colin Hynd we also did a concert of the songs.

[52] By the time Glen Lyon was released (2002, Footstompin CDFSR1714) it had very much become Martyn's project. He put countless hours of thought, work and creativity into it, and so, when he told me that he decided to leave my name off the 'Glen Lyon' CD cover I did not question the decision as I was in no doubt that he had done all the work on it—my voice was simply one instrument in his 'soundscape', part of his 'natural orchestra'. Nevertheless, it was probably not surprising some reviewers questioned it—*Dirty Linen*, (Aug/Sept 2002) concluded: 'Both Bennetts obviously love and respect these songs, with the result Margaret's singing is always front and centre: one wonders why this album is not credited to Margaret and Martyn Bennett. Still Martyn's skills as arranger, recordist, producer, and instrumentalist get a thorough workout without ever seeming to overwhelm the songs. The result is one of the most significant, interesting and powerful releases that either Bennett has been involved

with in their many combined years of music making. It's a refreshing album for anyone with an interest in Gaelic song.

[53] *Chaneil ubhlan idir agam, 'S ubhlan uil' aig cach, 'S ann tha m' ùbhal curaidh caineil, 'S cùl a chinn ri làr.* [I have no apple at all, When every one else has one, My sweet fragrant apple Lies with his head on the ground.] The apple was an analogy for the highest compliment that could be paid to a loved one.

[54] www.croftnofive.com

[55] Central to the track 'Liberation' on Grit, is Psalm 118, sung in Gaelic to the tune Coleshill, and 'lined out' by two sisters from the Isle of Lewis. The most striking vocal sound from Gaelic Scotland is arguably the metrical psalm with its surge of highly ornamented congregational singing. Unaccompanied and lined out by a 'precentor', the style dates to the 16th century. Unlike choral singing (with its strict discipline), there is absolutely no conductor and individuals are free to improvise as the spirit moves. Unusually, (especially for the time this psalm was recorded), it was sung by two women, and not a congregation led by a male precentor.

[56] Almost all the tracks with samples presented considerable challenge in ascertaining who owned the copyright then acquiring permission. On the one hand, the Lomax Archive in New York understood what he was doing ('Chanter' track 3) and gave clear guidelines for permission, but on the other hand, there were tracks that caused Martyn what seemed like endless frustration, distress and anguish—many issues emerged, not only of copyright but also of attitude and personality. The endless letters drained Martyn's energy (already very diminished by illness) and were equally demanding on Kirsten who carried much of the load and would go the last mile to help him through it. Suffice it to say, some of the correspondence at the time made grim reading.

[57] In 2004, Calum Martin began his psalm project by recording two CDs, *Salm*, vols I and II, in Back Free Church, Isle of Lewis. Martyn and Kirsten went to Lewis for the recording and to spend time with Calum and Yale Professor Willie Ruff who had travelled to Lewis

'It's Not the Time You Have...'

especially for the occasion. The 72-year old Alabama jazzman who, in previous years, shared gigs with Dizzy Gillespie, Duke Ellington and Miles Davies, was very excited to compare the Gaelic psalm singing to the 'lining out' he knew from the black church of his youth: "I have been to Africa many times in search of my cultural identity, but it was in the Highlands that I found the cultural roots of black America". Two unforgettable evenings of psalm singing were filmed by Eyeline Media for Channel 4, then in June 2004, Calum was invited to bring a group of Gaelic psalm singers to Liverpool to share a concert in the Cathedral with a choir black gospel singers from London. It would be difficult to imagine a bigger contrast in the churches, far less the traditions of the congregations—the Free Church is completely unadorned by crosses, statues or stained glass, while Liverpool Cathedral, the biggest Anglican cathedral in Europe, has magnificent architecture, stained glass windows, glorious statues and adornments. This concert was part of their 'Festival of the Voice' to celebrate the centenary of Liverpool Cathedral. Calum invited me to sing with the group and I was so inspired by the experience that I proposed to Colin Hynd that Celtic Connections Festival might have a concert of psalms and gospel in Glasgow Cathedral. It was only after a visit to Alabama later that year (again to sing psalms) that we experienced the even more exciting dynamic of singing with the black congregation that I suggested to Colin this should be 'it'—the concert in Glasgow, 'Salm and Soul' (now a CD) was held at Celtic Connections, 2005, with Calum Martin leading the singers from Lewis and the Revd Docaray Ingram leading the singers from Alabama. (It had been one of Martyn's dreams to be able to be at that concert, to hear the singing for himself, but by then he was too ill. Docary Ingram did, however, visit him twice and they shared some wonderful moments together the week before Martyn died.) When Calum produced the CD, he dedicated 'Salm and Soul' to Martyn. www.gaelicpsalmsinging.com

[58]   Manon met Martyn in 1999 when her village ran a celebration, *'Homage aux premiers arrivants écossaises'* [a homage to the first Scottish settlers], and invited Martyn and me to play and sing; we in turn asked Tony MacManus. It was in her native Quebec that Manon first heard Gaelic songs, a Gaelic psalm, the music of the bagpipes and fiddle and heard Martyn playing for a wild hyped-up *'dannsa rathaid'* [a

Lewis style, cross-roads dance, only it was held on a covered bridge in Quebec]. www.manonroussophotographe.com

[59]   They never climbed together, as my father, who, in my childhood of the 1950s had been a member of the Skye Mountain Rescue Team, emigrated to Canada in 1967.

[60]   R. Murray Schafer, *The New Soundscape: A Handbok for the Modern Music Teacher,* (Bernandol Music, Toronto, 1969) The same comments were apparently made after the première of Wagner's *Tristan,* Stravinsky's *Sacre,* Varèsé's *Poème électronique:* "Yes, but is it music?" My father sent the book to Martyn in 1994 with a letter on the inside cover: 'I think you might like this little book; although I have had it in my possession for nearly twenty years (since 1974) I still find pleasure in re-reading... (etc), Have fun! Love, Papi.'

[61]   Those familiar with Gordon Duncan's tunes will hear the familiar ring of Gordon's tune title 'Just for Seumus', composed for the recognised guru of bagpipes, Seamus McNeill when he disagreed with, and criticised, this wonderfully imaginative, talented and gloriously irreverent maverick of the pipes who will also be remembered with warm affection.

[62]   'Peace to your soul and a stone on your cairn' (*Scottish Customs from the Cradle to the Grave,* p. 306).

'It's Not the Time You Have...'

'It's Not the Time You Have...'

'Marvellous in our eyes...
                    Psalm 118—'Liberation' (Grit)

Go free, my son,
For all our love, we may not keep you as you were with us,
Nor would we now,
Not now the word is clear
That we remain and you may go.
We humbly lay your body in the earth,
This land from whence your mortal fathers came,
We briefly grieve
The shape you wore will change among these shining hills
But briefly
Grieve
For you are free
While we remain
Our duty still to do.
Fly free my son, fly free
And surely find
That which we prayed for with you.
Pray for still
God's will
Be done: my son
Far out in front of us you fly.
We are the children left behind
With love you gave us
Now to teach us
This day, always.
We are one,
Here to be free
As you my son.

                               Robert Urquhart, 1974
                         Courtesy of Jean Urquhart, 2006

Notes